The Past Master's Handbook

A Freemason's Guide to Modern Business Practices

Robert W. Howard, Jr.
Arjit S. Mahal

An indispensable resource for all Lodge officers.

A Past Master's Handbook: A Freemason's Guide to Modern Business Practices

Copyright © 2025 Crossroads Publishing, LLC

ALL RIGHTS RESERVED:

Crossroads Publishing, LLC does not grant you rights to resell or distribute this book without prior written consent of both Crossroads Publishing, LLC and the copyright owner of this book. This book may not be used for anything AI related, training, creating, etc. The authors have approved the final PDF of this book. With the exception of templates found in Section V to be used by Freemason Lodges, no part of this book may be reproduced or transmitted in any form or by any means, electronic or mechanical, including photocopying, recording, or by any information storage and retrieval system, without written permission from the publisher, except for including brief quotations in a review.

Disclaimer: Neither Crossroads Publishing, LLC, or our authors will be responsible for repercussions to anyone who utilizes the subject of this book for illegal, immoral or unethical use.

The views expressed herein do not necessarily reflect that of the publisher.

Crossroads Publishing, LLC

620-204-1710

www.crossroadspublishingllc.com

ISBN: 979-8-9999528-3-7

Authors—Robert W. Howard, Jr. and Arjit S. Mahal

Cover Design—Gabriel Georgeian

Editor—Tonya Andrews

Table of Contents

FOUNDATIONS – SECTION I 1
Purpose: 1
Introduction: 1
    What is a Past Master? 7
    The Worshipful Master, Past Master Alliance 8
    Immediate Past Master (IPM) 10
Background 11
Past Master's Framework 14
    Expected Results 15
    Buiding Principles for Role of Past Masters 18

CRITICAL TOOLS – SECTION II 20
Module 1 - Basic Facilitation Skills 21
Module 1a – Listening Skills 30
Module 1b – Promotion Skills 34
Module 2 – After Action Review 42
Module 3 – Masonic Motivation 48
Module 4a – Engaged Past Masters & Brethren 53
Module 4b – Committee Charter 54

TOOLS to Use Anytime – SECTION III 59
Module 5 - Assessed Gaps, Opportunities, and Remedies 60
Module 5a – Lodge Performance Measures 62
Module 5b - SWOT Analysis 67
Module 5c - SPOT Analysis 70
Module 5d – Project Management 72

ADDED VALUE – SECTION IV 78
General areas where the IPM/PM can help the Worshipful Master and the Lodge 78
Developing a Culture of Enlightenment in the Lodge 79
Getting Started in Your Lodge 87

TEMPLATES - SECTION V 88
Basic Facilitation Skills 89
Statement of Work (SOW) 90
Running Order Agenda (ROA) 91
Participants' Agenda 92

- Listening Ladder 93
- Promotion Skills 94
- After Action Review 95
- Masonic Motivation 96
- Committee Charter 97
- Lodge Performance Measures 98
- SWOT Analysis 99
- SPOT Analysis 101
- Project Management 102

- Works Cited 103
- Notes 104
- Authors... 112

Dedication

This Handbook is dedicated to the Spirit of Freemasonry as inspired by those great men, who throughout history carried the torch of knowledge and passed it down to us. We draw our inspiration from men such as King Solomon, who collaborated with his Phoenician neighbors to build a temple following the designs provided by the Grand Architect of the Universe. King Athelstan was the first king to rule over the whole of England. According to Masonic tradition, it was his son Edwin who called a General Assembly at York in the year 926 to revise deficiencies within the operative craft and establish a new constitution. It would be Wiliam Shaw in the year 1598, who established the first of his statutes for the governance of modern masonry. He is the one responsible for giving us the basic structure of our Masonic Lodges. Then, of course, there was John Theophilus Desaguliers, who contributed greatly to the Age of Enlightenment, who was the prime mover behind the formation of the Grand Lodge of London and Westminster and is credited with giving us modern Freemasonry.

The authors of this book have dedicated many decades each to the Masonic Craft. They were both influenced and initiated into the Craft by their respective fathers, who themselves were inspired by those generations of Masons who carried the torch of enlightenment before them.

In addition to the rich knowledge and wisdom transferred from these previous generations, their character was further shaped by ritual, tradition and the numerous Brethren who mentored and coached them every step of their Masonic careers, enabling them to serve the cause of Freemasonry's noble tenants.

With gratitude,

Robert W. Howard, Jr.

Arjit S. Mahal

Acknowledgements

Most Worshipful Omar Morris, Grand Master, The Grand Lodge of Free and Accepted Masons; for the State of New Jersey for all the inspiration he provided in the advancement of Masonic enlightenment.

Worshipful Brother Jeff Challinor, Past Provincial Grand Superintendent of Works, Provence of Cheshire, The United Grand Lodge of England; for his contribution to the role of the Immediate Past Master.

Right Worshipful Kulwant Singh, Past Deputy Grand Master, The Grand Lodge of Ancient, Free & Accepted Masons of India; for his years of friendship and encouragement.

Worshipful Brother Gene Fucetola, The Grand Lodge of New Jersey; for his advice and input in the production of this book.

Mr. Micheal Foresman, for his assistance in the production of the graphics and illustrations.

Disclaimer: This book is the culmination of diligent research that reflects input from numerous sources and Jurisdictions. Nothing contained herein should be construed as reflecting the policy of any particular Grand Lodge.

Preface

Before we proceed, it is important to discuss what it is about Freemasonry that makes it so special and what it is that induces its members to work so willingly to support their community and give aid to a Brother Mason.

If you ask a Freemason his impression of the Craft, he might simply say, "Its purpose is to make good men better." It is through ritual, symbols, and allegory that Masonry teaches its lessons in morality and conduct, and promotes Brotherly Love, Relief, and Truth. As a Mason progresses through the fraternity in a quest for self-improvement, his positive influence will be felt in the community, thereby making the world that much better.

"Whenever or wherever people are in need, Masons are there to help."
~ Brother Norman Vincent Peale

What Value Does Freemasonry Provide to Its Members?

A Rich Heritage – The Freemasons honor and share their connection with 300 years of history, 600 years of heritage, 1000 years of tradition, 3000 years of legend, and 6000 years of enlightenment. Employing Freemasonry's ancient heritage together with the symbolism of architecture, like-minded men help impart awareness and knowledge to build character, one Brother at a time.

The **300 years of history** references the year of the formation of the Grand Lodge of England in 1717. Respectively, **600 years of heritage** references Speculative Masonry taking its roots in the form of craft lodges in the 15th Century. The first written reference to Mason's Lodge is in records of the Aberdeen Lodge in Scotland on June 27, 1483. Considering the **one thousand years of tradition** reference, it is the period of the 10th and 11th Centuries when the Operative Masons formed guilds and worked on the cathedrals of Europe. The **3000 years of legend** reference is the building of King Solomon's temple around 1000 BC. Finally, the **6000 years of enlightenment** references the Masonic allegory, which identifies Adam as the first Freemason and his birth marking the first year of light, (*Anno Lucis*).

Stonemasons at work, a carving in marble, Florence, Italy. (Picture Courtesy Arjit Mahal).

Valuable Tenets – Through self-reflection and the pursuit of understanding the "Design" of the Grand Architect of the Universe, Brethren strive to exemplify the tenets of Freemasonry in all aspects of their lives. These include Brotherly Love, Relief, and Truth.

- *Brotherly Love* - Helps us promote and foster social and benevolent affection.
- *Relief* - The virtue of unselfish service to one another.
- *Truth* - Conveys our understanding of ourselves and our spiritual connection with the Divine.

Philosophical Enrichment – Freemasonry promotes philosophical enrichment among its members and education through studying our ancient origins and many philosophical, esoteric, non-secular, theosophical, sociological beliefs and schools of thought. We foster a universal Brotherhood based on the moral foundation and commonalities that link all men. This is the true essence of our fraternity.

Life Skills - By actively participating in Lodge activities, Freemasonry allows its members to learn and develop critical skills, including leadership, public speaking, relationship building, organizational awareness, and management. These skills are transferable to one's personal and professional life.

Refined Character – Overall, Masonic experiences have the effect of helping transform a good man into a better human being and an asset to the local and world community.

It is hoped that by sharing the tools and techniques covered in this book with the Masonic community, Masons will be in a better position to advance the pure principles of the fraternity and continue to perpetuate its values through the ages.

FOUNDATIONS – SECTION I

Purpose:

There are many landmark books that have been written over the years, which do a good job of unravelling much of the symbolism and allegory found buried in our ritual and founding documents. Whereas these resources provide a strong foundation for our Craft, what we need today is a how-to manual that can provide an up-and-coming Lodge officer with the tools and resources required to develop an organization and lead his Brethren to a common goal. Whereas previous generations may have relied on men, who have had a wealth of experience gleaned from a lifetime working in business and government to lead the Lodge, today's Mason comes from a more diverse group of professions. This requires him to learn organizational development and management skills concurrently with his development as a Lodge officer.

However, due to shrinking membership and changing circumstances, today's Mason is more-or-less being pushed through the chairs and spends most of his energy just keeping up with learning ritual and conferring degrees. Therefore, it may not be possible for him to learn the managements skills necessary to run a Lodge until he has actually left the East.

So, in today's world, where Brothers are rushing to the East, it is the Past Master who has the available time to focus on Lodge management. It is hoped that Brethren will begin to see the role of Past Master as a valuable resource within the Lodge.

Just as any other "officer" needs to prepare for his role, this book provides the tools and resources to arm the Past Master in the execution of his responsibilities.

Introduction:

Whereas there are many events and traditions which have influenced the formation of Freemasonry, we can credit William Shaw with providing us with the basic framework for the modern Lodge. Shaw was Master of Works under James VI of Scotland. James ruled during a relatively tumultuous time when the British Isles would be grappling with evolving protestant sects in the face of traditional Catholicism. One of his long-lasting contributions to this struggle was his revision of the bible. In fact, he might be best known for the King James Bible, which is today the most popular version of the bible and can be found on the altar of Lodges throughout the English-speaking world.

Perhaps his greatest contribution to our Gentle Craft was his appointment of William Shaw to oversee and maintain all royal castles and palaces. As Master of Works and General Warden of the master stonemasons, he would introduce a structure to the running of operative stonemason lodges, which has transferred to our Speculative Lodges.

On December 28, 1598, Shaw published his first set of statutes and ordinances, which were to govern all master masons within the kingdom. Since the Shaw Statutes would have the full force of law, each lodge was motivated to scrupulously adhere to these standards. Most notable within these statutes was the requirement that each lodge incorporate a hierarchy of masters, wardens and deacons. Just as important to the modern Freemason's Lodge, these statutes required a written record and accounting of its membership. This would open the door to the significant role of the secretary in the smooth operation of every lodge, whether operative or speculative.

Shaw's second set of statutes were published on December 28, 1599. These statutes were more legalistic and empowered the lodge of Edinburgh as the principal lodge in Scotland. It is worth noting that both sets of Shaw's statues were recorded in the minutes of Edinburgh Lodge No. 1 and can be viewed there today in their original handwritten text. In spite of the improved level of organization that was provided by the Shaw Statutes, they fall short of providing the necessary tools for the operations of a modern Freemason's Lodge.

Although, the roots of modern Freemasonry were clearly planted in Scottish soil, we cannot ignore the fact that the Grand Lodge of London and Westminster has claimed prominence by establishing the first enduring Grand Lodge. One of the outcomes of this Grand Lodge was the publication in 1723 of *The Constitutions of the Freemasons* by James Anderson, a Scotsman from Aberdeen working under the auspices of this new English Grand Lodge. Within its pages, this document would, through its allegorical use of the stone mason's lodge, provide some hints for the running of the Speculative Lodge.

Please note: The following is taken directly from Anderson's work in the chapter entitled, 'The Charges of a Freemason' and is shown using the same archaic language as was found in the original publication.

> ### *V. Of the Management of the CRAFT in working.*
>
> *All Masons shall work honestly on working Days, that they may live creditably on holy Days; and the time appoint ed by the Law of the Land, or confirm'd by Custom, shall be observ'd.*
>
> *The most expert of the Fellow-Craftsmen shall be chosen or appointed the Master, or Overseer of the Lord's Work; who is to be call'd MASTER by those that work under him. The Craftsmen are to avoid all ill Language, and to call each other by no disobliging Name, but Brother or Fellow; and to behave themselves courteously within and without the Lodge.*
>
> *The Master, knowing himself to be able of Cunning, shall undertake the Lord's Work as reasonably as possible, and truly dispend his Goods as if they were his own; nor to give more Wages to any Brother or Apprentice than he re ally may deserve.*
>
> *Both the MASTER and the Masons receiving their Wages justly, shall be faithful to the Lord, and honestly fin ish their Work, whether Ta sk or Journey. Nor put the Work to Task that hath been accustomed to Journey.*

> *None shall discover Envy at the Prosperity of a Brother, nor supplant him or put him out of his Work, if he be capable to finish the same; for no Man can finish another's Work so much to the Lord's Profit, unless he be thoroughly acquainted with the Design and Draughts of him that began it.*
>
> *When a Fellow-Craftsman is chosen Warden of the Work under the Master, he shall be true both to Master and Fellows, shall carefully oversee the Work in the Master's Absence to the Lord's Profit; and his Brethren shall obey him.*
>
> *All Masons employ'd, shall meekly receive their Wages without Murmuring or Mutiny, and not desert the Master till the Work is finish'd.*
>
> *A younger Brother shall be instructed in working, to prevent spoiling the Materials for want of Judgment, and for encreasing and continuing of Brotherly Love.*
>
> *All the Tools used in working shall be approved by the Grand Lodge.*
>
> *No Labourer shall be employ'd in the proper Work of Masonry; nor shall Free-Masons work with those that are not free, without an urgent Necessity; nor shall they teach Labourers and unaccepted Masons, as they should teach a Brother or Fellow*

According to Anderson, the elements of this section were extracted from the ancient charges. Whereas the adherence to these principles would appeal to the good character of its members, it did little to guide its members through the governance of the Freemason's Lodge. On the other hand, such guidance may have, in fact, been considered superfluous at the time. This was due to many of its early members calling on their own experience as scientists, businessmen, and statesmen to ensure the success of a well-run Lodge.

As time progressed and the scope of men joining Lodges expanded, so did the ritual. It would be within the ritual itself that we would begin to see some guidance on how the Lodge should be structured, together with the role of its officers. Just as an example, we will take a look at the *Masonic Manual and Code, 1947* of the Grand Lodge of Free and Accepted Masons of Georgia. This popular book, originally published in 1915, was used by generations of Masons to guide them through the operations of the Lodge. In its installation ritual, it specifies moral lessons as well as the duties of each Lodge officer. The following are examples of the duties as outlined in this valuable resource:

Worshipful Master – The Brother to be installed as the Worshipful Master is expected to be qualified for his position as well as a man of good moral and great skill. He promises to impart Masonic Light to the Brethren and preserve the Landmarks, Traditions and symbols of Freemasonry. In addition to his obligation, the incoming Master agrees to conform to the Ancient Charges, which include the following admonitions:

I. You agree to be a good man and true, and strictly to obey the moral law.

II. You agree to be a peaceable citizen, and cheerfully to conform to the laws of the country in which you reside.

III. You promise not to be concerned in plots and conspiracies against the government, but patiently to submit to the decisions of the constituted authorities.

IV. You agree to pay a proper respect to the civil magistrates, to work diligently, live creditably and act honorably by all men.

V. You agree to hold in veneration the original rulers and patrons of the Order of Masonry, and their regular successors, supreme and subordinate, according to their stations, and to submit to the awards and resolutions of your brethren, in Lodge convened, in every case consistent with the constitutions of the Order.

VI. You agree to avoid private piques and quarrels, and to guard against intemperance and excess.

VII. You agree to be cautious in your behavior, courteous to your brethren and faithful to your Lodge.

VIII. You promise to respect genuine brethren, and to discourage imposters and all dissenters from the original plan of Masonry.

IX. You agree to promote the general good of society, to cultivate the social virtues, and to propagate the knowledge of the mystic art.

X. You promise to pay homage to the Grand Master for the time being, and to his officers when duly installed; and strictly to conform to every edict of the Grand Lodge, or General Assembly of Masons, that is not subversive of the principles and groundwork of Masonry.

XI. You admit that it is not in the power of any man, or body of men, to make any innovations in the body of Masonry.

XII. You promise a regular attendance on the committees and communications of the Grand Lodge, on receiving proper notice; and to pay attention to all the duties of Masonry, on convenient occasions.

XIII. You admit that no new Lodge can be formed without permission of the Grand Lodge; and that no countenance is given to any irregular Lodge, or to any person clandestinely initiated therein, being contrary to the Ancient Charges of the Order.

XIV. You admit that no person can be regularly made a Mason in, or admitted a member of, any regular Lodge, without previous notice and due inquiry into his character.

XV. You agree that no visitors shall be received into your Lodge without due examination and producing proper vouchers for their having been initiated into a regular Lodge.

Beyond the obligation, the above admonitions and the moral lessons specifically directed to the Worshipful Master, the following is a list of items he is directed to keep and maintain, *i.e.*:

- The Book of Constitutions - to be searched at all times and read to the Lodge.
- The Lodge charter - to be carefully preserved.
- The By-Laws - to be carefully and punctually executed.

Only in this very last section, do we begin to see some general guidance, which provides some minimal direction for the Worshipful Master towards the governance of his Lodge.

Whereas many Jurisdictions will have officers with different names and slightly different duties, the following are examples of duties assigned to the Lodge officers during their installation in the Jurisdiction of the Grand Lodge of Georgia:

Senior Warden – Your regular attendance on our stated meetings is essentially necessary. In the absence of the Master, you are to govern this Lodge; in his presence, you are to assist him in the government of it.

Junior Warden – To you is committed the superintendence of the Lodge during the hours of refreshment; it is therefore, indispensably necessary, that you should not only be temperate and discreet, in the indulgence of your own inclinations, but to see that none convert the hours of refreshment into intemperance or excess. Your regular and punctual attendance is particularly requested.

Treasurer - It is your duty to receive all money from the Secretary, to keep a just and true account of the same and to pay them out on the order of the Lodge with the consent of the Worshipful Master.

Secretary - It is your duty to keep a correct account of the proceedings of the Lodge, proper to be written, to collect all moneys and pay them over to the Treasurer, taking his receipt therefor.

Chaplain - It is your duty to perform those solemn services which we should constantly render to our infinite Creator, and which, when offered by one may, whose is "to point to heaven and lead the way," may, by refining our souls, strengthening our virtues and purifying our minds, prepare us for admission into the society of those above, whose happiness will be as endless as it is perfect.

Senior Deacons - You are to welcome and provide for the examination of visiting brethren, to carry all messages from the Worshipful to the Senior Warden and elsewhere as you may be directed, to attend to the Holy Altar, to attend alarms at the inner door and to receive and conduct candidates.

Junior Deacons – It is your duty to see that the Lodge is duly tiled, to attend to all alarms at the outer door, and to carry all messages from the Senior Warden to the Worshipful Master and elsewhere as you may be directed.

Stewarts - It is your duty to cope the Holy Altar, to superintend the preparation of candidates, to introduce them into the Lodge and to assist the Junior Warden in the duties of his office.

Tiler - As the sword is placed in the hands of the Tyler to enable him effectually to keep off all cowans and eavesdroppers, and to see that none enter unless duly qualified and having the permission of the Worshipful Master.

The Brethren - You will have but one aim: to please each other, to unite in the grand designs of being happy, and to communicate happiness.

In addition to the installation ceremony, we may hear many of these duties reviewed and repeated at every meeting. The point of showing them here is to demonstrate that while the ritual and founding documents do provide some basic information concerning the role of the officers, they actually provide very little guidance on how the Worshipful Master and his officers can contribute to the functioning of the Lodge. In other words, the Craft tends to provide its officers with very little in terms of guidance to run a successful Lodge. Instead, it would be the background, experience and imagination of its officers that would account for the success of a well-run Lodge. Most Masons, who have been around, have seen the ebbs and flows that occur when certain Brethren enter or leave key positions. Just as in 1723, when Anderson's Constitutions were published, it tends to be the talents and experience provided by a few key officers that drive the success of the Lodge.

Whether it is scouting, church, veteran groups or Freemasonry, we are living in a world where people are just not joining organizations in the numbers that they have in the past. As a result, Lodge membership is diminishing, and men assume the oriental chair with less experience than Brethren of years past. In short, Worshipful Masters and other Lodge officers may move to positions of authority without the experience necessary to do more than the bare minimum, when it comes to running a Lodge. Therefore, to be successful in our role as Worshipful Master, we now find it necessary to supplement our experience level with resources designed to inform, educate and prepare us for Lodge management.

The bulk of this book will focus on providing concrete steps to run a successful Lodge.

Through the following sections, we will explore the tools and resources that any Mason can employ to strengthen his Lodge and even add value to his community.

What is a Past Master?

Modern Freemasonry, as it is known today, has existed for over three hundred years. The systems and protocols for running a Lodge have been handed down from Past Master to Worshipful Master for generations. The older Past Masters of today would have been influenced by venerable Past Masters from decades in the past and they would themselves have been influenced by those from yet another era.

Therefore, in a very true sense the Past Master is the Worshipful Master's very link to the early years of Freemasonry.

The running of a Lodge, the conferring of degrees and the planning of collation have gone on year to year, relatively unchanged. There is likely no scenario that can challenge a Worshipful Master today, that has not been addressed by a Worshipful Master in years past. Therefore, the Past Master should be seen as an invaluable asset to be used by the Worshipful Master.

Before we discuss the important relationship that should exist between the Worshipful Master and the Past Masters, let's talk about the development of a Past Master. In a very true sense, a Past Master's development starts well before he became a Mason. To be given entry into the Craft, he will have already had standards and a strong sense of morality through a belief in God. He may have already been involved in social organizations such as a school club, a house of worship or a sports team; additionally, he likely had the responsibility of holding down a job to support himself or his family. Even if he didn't realize it at the time, he learned how to interact with different people, set goals and solve problems built on a foundation of morality.

At some point, he likely asked a friend to recommend him to be made a Mason. Once he was voted into the Lodge, he would go through a series of hierarchal degrees. Like building blocks, one degree was built on the principles and lessons of the earlier degrees. The primary lesson of the Entered Apprentice degree is to understand the importance of maintaining confidentiality among and between the Brethren. This important first step of the Past Master in training allows him to truly get to know his Brothers, to discuss sensitive topics and not fear that information will spread beyond the group.

The Fellow Craft Degree emphasizes that one must take on the responsibility to learn and develop as a man and a Mason. It is his responsibility to learn the lessons of the degrees and apply them to his own life both in and out of the Lodge. The more he learns through the ritual and Masonic history, the stronger he will become as a man and the more he will contribute to the Lodge.

Among the many lessons of the Master Mason degree, he is admonished to abide by the constitution and laws of the Grand Lodge, but more importantly to protect the integrity of the Craft. He will then go on to participate in the ritual of the Lodge, occupy many of its stations and places, and participate in committees necessary for the administration of the Lodge.

The Brethren of the Lodge, recognizing the skills he has developed and the contribution he has made to the Lodge, will elect him to the exalted chair once occupied by King Solomon himself. He is now eligible to take the oath of a Past Master, which has its own obligation, grips, and words. The point we make here is that a Past Master is more than a Brother, who once served in the East; through the Past Master Degree, he retains a certain status, which sets him apart from the other Brethren of the Lodge.

So, in a very real sense, as a Past Master, only now are you prepared to complete your journey, because now you have *all* the tools that the Craft has to offer. It is therefore incumbent upon the Past Master to keep learning and growing, so that he can continue to develop as a Mason, while giving back to his Lodge. Concurrently, the Worshipful Master must understand that the Past Masters have a wealth of knowledge available for the asking. For the sake of a well-run Lodge, it is essential that the Master takes advantage of this invaluable resource.

The incoming Master must remember that he is not expected to rebuild his Lodge from the ground up or solve every problem on his own. If he enlists the assistance of the Past Masters to manage some of the routine functions of the Lodge, he will be better enabled to advance his own program and put his unique stamp upon the history of the Lodge. The Worshipful Master should also keep in mind that he will be likely facing some of the same problems that have challenged Masters throughout the centuries. So, it is likely that a Past Master will have the experience to easily address a problem that, at first glance, may seem overwhelming.

The Worshipful Master, Past Master Alliance

When a Brother, who has never before presided in the East is about to be installed as Worshipful Master, he will have the degree of Past Master conferred upon him. In the ceremony, which obligates him as a Past Master, he vows not to reveal the secrets applying to his chair to anyone but a Brother Past Master. This is not just a quaint artifact from the ancient past, but a necessary admonition that is quite relevant. It addresses the fact that the dynamics of running a Lodge can only be fully appreciated by another Past Master, who has been entangled in the same problems or faced the same challenges. If he thinks back to his obligation, he might be reminded of *Ecclesiastes 4:12 (KJV),* where he is admonished not to go it alone, *i.e.:*

"And if one prevails against him, two shall withstand him; and a threefold cord is not quickly broken."

This verse reminds us that we should be willing to accept the support and assistance of friends, who may be in a position to help us.

In the profane world for example, it is quite common for leaders to keep council with others, who are at the same level. When people, with comparable experiences and similar challenges address an issue, an optimal result can be obtained in a most expeditious manner.

A successful Worshipful Master will therefore surround himself with some of those Past Masters who have been responsible for the success and growth of the Lodge. By tapping into this resource, the Worshipful Master may be able to address some particularly tough issues, since these Past Masters likely have faced some of the same issues during their tenure in the East. This is not to say that he will keep anything from the Brethren, just that when he does bring something before the Lodge it has been well-thought out with a high probability of a good outcome. A caucus of Past Masters can likely dispose of a sticky situation more easily than a full-blown debate with all the Brethren of the Lodge.

As he continues to grow and learn, the Past Master should identify the gaps in his base of knowledge and develop some competency in those areas. But just as important, he should fully appreciate the duties and responsibilities of the Worshipful Master and prepare himself to act as a resource in the areas where the Worshipful Master may need some help. Below are some of the duties and responsibilities of the Worshipful Master; the Past Master should prepare himself to jump in as needed.

- He represents the Lodge at the Grand Lodge.
- He is responsible for scheduling Lodge functions.
- He performs Degree and Ritual work.
- He updates the Lodge By-Laws as necessary.
- He oversees the financial issues of the Lodge as necessary.
- He takes time in learning various Masonic allegories and symbols, and he shares his knowledge with others.
- He educates the Brethren.
- He delegates duties to Lodge committees.
- He delegates duties to Lodge officials.
- He is responsible for the Trestle board communication.
- He is in charge of the maintenance of Lodge regalia.

In addition to the support he will have from his Wardens and Past Masters, the Worshipful Master should seek out a specific mentor from among the Past Masters. Finding a mentor is something one can do early on in his Masonic career. As he travels to Lodges throughout his District and Jurisdiction or even within his own Lodge, he should keep his eyes open for those whom he wishes to emulate.

However, we should keep in mind that mentoring is not an informal or casual relationship. Securing a mentor can be achieved by identifying someone we respect and then having a conversation with him to ask if he would like to be our mentor. The Past Master mentor will need to meet with his protege' on a regular basis and impart specific advice related to running a Lodge. In exchange, the protégé' will need to add value to the relationship and this means the protégé' will need to identify something of value that he can impart to the Past Master mentor. The protégé' might be adept at ritual, Masonic history or planning social events. In this case, the protégé' can participate in a degree at his mentor's Lodge, give a presentation or partner with his Lodge in planning a social event. If the Past Master mentor is from his own Lodge, the Worshipful Master should make sure the mentor is given credit for all he has and will continue to contribute to the Lodge.

Finally, whether you are a Worshipful Master seeking assistance, a Past Master developing his skills or a venerable Brother considering a protégé, we should be reminded that learning and mentoring are all *part and parcel* of Freemasonry. In fact, some of the luminaries of Freemasonry have emphasized this in their writings.

For example, this direct quote from William Preston says the following:

And, as a last general recommendation, let me exhort you to dedicate yourself to such pursuits as may enable you to become at once respectable in your rank of life; useful to mankind; and an ornament to the Society of which you have this day been admitted a member; that you would more especially devote your leisure hours to the study of such of the liberal arts and sciences as may lie within the compass of your attainment; and that, without neglecting the ordinary duties of your station, you would consider yourself called upon to make a daily advancement in Masonic knowledge.

Thomas Smith Webb provides us with the following memorable reminder in this direct quote:

At your leisure hours, that you may improve in masonic knowledge, you are to converse with well-informed brethren, who will be always as ready to give, as you will be ready to receive.

Immediate Past Master (IPM)

In some Jurisdictions, the IPM may be awarded a jewel and be assigned a chair directly next to the Worshipful Master. He is thus positioned, so that he might whisper sage council in the Master's ear during the meeting. Whereas other jurisdictions do not have such a station in their regular communications, it is always acceptable for the Worshipful Master to invite any Past Master to the East. A few well-placed words can keep the meeting on track, while avoiding ***typical*** pitfalls.

It should also be noted that in some jurisdictions, there are typically enough seats in the East to accommodate a number of sitting Masters and Past Masters.

As a Past Master, your role is to help assist and support the Worshipful Master in the smooth running of the Lodge. Remember, he's the boss and your mission is to support him. You must resist the temptation to build your own power base or detract from the prestige of the Master.

Even if a seat is not provided for the IPM in the East, there will be plenty of opportunities for the Worshipful Master to tap into the wealth of knowledge and experience held by the Past Masters during his Masonic year. Just as the Master has the support of his Wardens, he will always be able to lean on the Past Masters for support.

Background

In years past, a typical Lodge might easily have had 50 or more of its members regularly attending its communications. Within this number, there could have been 10 to 15 Past Masters, each of whom may have had a particular competency or passion, which would be useful in supporting Lodge operations. Today, we are now finding that after the term of a Worshipful Master concludes, in many cases, he just "fades away." Given today's low attendance levels, we are missing this invaluable Lodge asset and must take affirmative steps to fill this void. By fully appreciating the value of the Past Master, we can likely find a solution to this ongoing problem.

Additionally, however, there are other concerns that come to play when Lodge attendance is low. It is an unfortunate reality that today the Worshipful Master of the Lodge may only be marginally trained as a Mason and as a leader. As a result, he may have less passion for his role as he is pushed into chairs for which he may not be properly prepared. In the end, he may just burn out avoiding future involvement in the Lodge as the process starts a new with the next generation of new Masons.

In earlier days, when Lodges were packed, it was possible for a new Master Mason to slowly assimilate into the Lodge. The position of Lodge Steward was an easy way to observe rituals, get to know the Brethren and become familiar with the workings of the Lodge. At a minimum, a new Master Mason could expect to have a relatively casual role lasting two years.

With so many Brethren working their way up the line, there was ample opportunity for young Masons to enjoy some of the special roles that the Craft had to offer. For Jurisdictions, that have Masters of Ceremonies, there is an opportunity to establish your first formal relationship with a man as he becomes a Mason. Here you will have to commit to memory your first significant piece of ritual. At this point, if you move on to the Junior Deacon's Chair, you may have already experienced four or more years as a member of the Lodge.

Here, the Junior Deacon would need to start thinking about his future. Specifically, he should be thinking about his role as Senior Deacon. The Senior Deacon typically gives the Middle Chamber (or Step) lecture during the Fellow Craft degree. And, if this is your fifth year in the Craft with time to plan, this task can be approached without pressure. As you continue up the line, at an unrushed pace, there is plenty of opportunity to prepare yourself to confer the EA Degree as the Junior Warden, and the FC Degree as the Senior Warden, while learning to be King Solomon for your big year.

In reality, today's Worshipful Masters have skipped chairs in their rush to the East. Degrees depend on fill-ins from neighboring Lodges and ritual experts who are seen routinely around the District giving lectures. The unfortunate reality is that by the time you make it to IPM, you may not have the same level of competency and experience that Past Masters have had in the past.

Through this resource, we will identify various means of reinvigorating the Past Masters, to maintain his involvement in Lodge, but more importantly, give him additional opportunities to continue enjoying everything that Masonry has to offer.

The Past Master is uniquely positioned to provide the Lodge with a significant level of support. The moment he becomes the IPM or Junior Past Master, he no longer has the pressure of directly running the Lodge. He can, therefore, take some of the burden off the Worshipful Master in any number of ways. In addition to areas of ritual, mentoring and Lodge administration, the IPM can begin to focus on providing exciting and meaningful programs and activities, which could enrich the Lodge and improve the Masonic experience. To achieve these important goals, this book will provide the Past Masters with the skill, tools and understanding to support him in this role.

WORSHIPFUL MASTER LEADERSHIP SKILLS – Inspiration: *The Master's Book* by Carl Claudy

According to Carl Claudy, the Worshipful Master needs the attributes of a diplomat, financier, adviser, councilor, friend, critic and executive, while providing the Brethren with entertainment, instruction and inspiration at meetings, events and activities. This is a very high bar, and even in the best of circumstances, the Worshipful Master is going to need the help of the Past Masters. The Past Master should, therefore, be mindful of these attributes and, where the Worshipful Master may be lacking, prepare himself to fill in the gaps.

Remember, just as the Worshipful Master must delegate the work of the Lodge to his officers, each Past Master does not necessarily need to fill in the gaps all on his own. If a Past Master can motivate someone else to effectively do a job, he has provided a great service to the Lodge and is now that much more available to tackle something else.

Each Past Master should consider himself a friend and colleague of the Worshipful Master. Keep your eyes open and look for ways to make the Worshipful Master successful in everything he does. Remember that any advice or guidance you provide to the Worshipful Master should be given discreetly and in private. It is critical that the Brethren have confidence in, and respect for, the Worshipful Master.

As you proceed through this book, you will be given the tools and processes to manage your Lodge with the same resources used by corporations and executives. They are provided in simple terms and can be implemented by any Lodge officer with the goal of getting things accomplished in an effective manner.

The tools are broken down into individual modules, each with a specific focus. Once you have read through the modules, go back and find one that piques your interest and practice it until you get comfortable with it. You can then implement the principles of the module to see how it works in real-life situations. You will be amazed at how using proper business techniques will secure positive results.

With tools offered in this book, a Past Master will gain competency in the following areas:

- ➢ Mentoring (to the W.M.)
- ➢ Coaching (the W.M., P.M.s & the Brethren)
- ➢ Masonic Motivation (to the Lodge)
- ➢ Community Outreach

- Communications
- Measuring and Monitoring Progress

Specifically, the Past Master will be adding value in the following areas:

- Support and guide the new Worshipful Master to ensure that:
    - The Lodge maintains its competency in ritual.
    - Committees run efficiently.
    - The mentor program is being implemented.
    - New Masons are being integrated into the Lodge.

- Assess and recommend improvement of the Lodge for its effectiveness and sustainability.

- Oversee, champion, and facilitate:
    - Recruitment.
    - Attendance.
    - Job gaps.
    - Community involvement.

Past Master's Framework

You will find below, a Past Master's Framework, which depicts all the necessary tools to empower the Past Master and develop him as an invaluable asset to the Lodge. We will take you methodically through each tool in the framework and will start with providing you with the basic skill necessary to ensure effective communication. Next, we will give you some simple techniques that can be used to create a culture of continuous improvement within the Lodge.

You will learn real methods for improving the Lodge experience, while ensuring each of the Brethren are sufficiently challenged to keep them invigorated and involved. Further, by introducing you to additional tools used in every business environment, the Past Master will be armed with techniques that can be used anytime to ensure that every goal is met, and the Lodge delivers all that Freemasonry has to offer.

Finally, whereas these tools are essential for the running of a successful Lodge, the Brethren who apply these principles will learn that their application will benefit them in their professional lives as well. Whether a sales manager, or a pipefitter, a CEO or a shop foreman, the following are indispensable concepts for the success of any group or organization.

Past Master's Framework

	Tools	Outcomes
Critical Tools	1. Basic Facilitation Skills 　a) *Listening Skills* 　b) *Promotion Skills*	Building Consensus
	2. After Action Review	Optimal Continuous Improvement
	3. Masonic Motivation	Improved Masonic Experience, Engagement & Retention
	4. More Active & Higher Performing Lodge 　a) *Engaged Past Masters and Brethren* 　b) *Committee Charter* 　c) *Community Outreach*	Optimal Involvement in the Lodge & the Community
General Tools (Use Anytime)	5. Assessed Gaps, Opportunities & Remedies 　a) *Lodge Performance Measures* 　b) *SWOT Analysis* 　c) *SPOT Analysis* 　d) *Project Management*	Viable Programs for the Success of the Lodge

Expected Results

As we move through the Past Master's Framework and come to grips with the Past Master's role, we should make certain subtle but important distinctions. Whereas the *skills* covered in this book will provide you with the framework for success, it will be your *experience* in implementing these skills that will give you the *knowledge* to be a motivated and successful member of your Lodge. This is best illustrated by analyzing these elements separately.

Knowledge - learning happens when people can demonstrate that they **know** something they didn't know before. This includes facts as well as insights or realizations.

Skills - skills have been learned when people demonstrate that they can **do** something they couldn't do before or can do something better than they could previously.

Learning from experience - the process of acquiring knowledge and/or skills by **doing**. This is also known as experiential learning. This happens when one is motivated to always apply knowledge and skills of a given discipline which then becomes one's behavior. Studies have shown that you learn 10% from formal training, 20% from others such as coaches and mentors, and 70% by doing.

Becoming an effective Past Master is, therefore, a combination of knowledge, skill and experience. Whereas this book will cover the skill you will require to be effective, it is up to you to be motivated to gain the experience to make a difference. As we move forward, let's keep the following formula in mind:

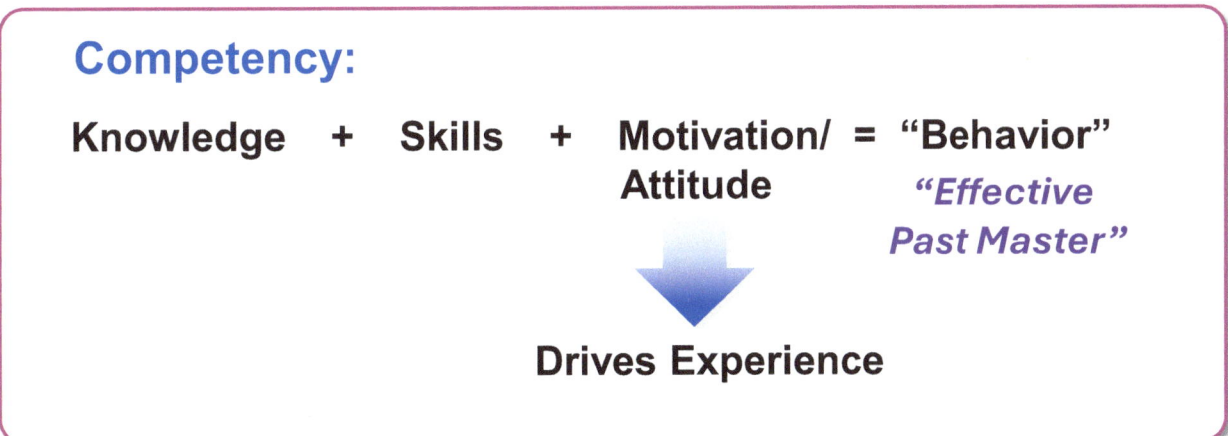

To make the point, we will look at a short example. Imagine a new Master Mason steps into the role of Lodge Treasurer. Let's assume that in his professional life, he is an experienced bookkeeper. He clearly has the *skill* to maintain the accounts of the Lodge. However, what he lacks is the *knowledge* pertaining to Lodge operations, Standard Operating Procedures (SOP) and Grand Lodge regulations. He must get involved and become acquainted with protocols previously established by the Lodge and reporting requirements of the Grand Lodge. To do this, he may need to do some research and even consult other Lodge Treasurers, who are likely to have a wealth of experience. In short, learning a skill is only a part of the formula to be effective in any role.

To develop competency with the skills and tools identified to become a successful Past Master will take substantial effort, time, and experience. Therefore, the reader needs to diligently find opportunities to practice them.

The following is a summary of the basic skills and tools we will be covering in this book:

Basic Facilitation Skills
Directing any group or committee to achieve a common goal is a learned skill. By employing the skills covered below, a facilitator or committee chair will more likely be in a position to fulfill the mission of the Lodge or committee. Therefore, by honing one's facilitation skills, we are able to optimize planning and communications without leaving anything to chance.

Listening Skills
An effective facilitator must hone his communications skills and in particular become a good listener. Like any skill, it must be learned and has specific elements, which should be taken to heart. One important way to ensure you are a good listener is to employ "active listening." This technique will not only ensure that there are no misunderstandings relative to what was just communicated but, if used correctly, will help you build a congenial rapport with the speaker.

Promotion Skills
Communicating your thoughts effectively is an indispensable trait for any facilitator. How you make your point and what you include in your communications will determine, to a great extent, how well your proposals will be received. Therefore, by taking the time to learn some simple techniques, the facilitator will be better armed to interact with the Brethren or any other stakeholders within the community.

After Action Review (AAR)
By analyzing the results of any activity and following every event with an AAR, no matter how small, the participants can identify what worked and what didn't work and thereby be prepared to do a better job the next time the activity is planned. This simple process will create a culture of continuous improvement within the Lodge.

Masonic Motivation
Just like anything else, finding the means of improving the Masonic experience in your Lodge, engaging your members and retaining your experienced past masters, requires the use of tried-and-true techniques. One process is identified below, which will give a Lodge options for keeping its Lodge members motivated and retaining those who may be vulnerable to "burnout."

More Active and Higher Performing Lodge
Among the traditional committees that most Lodges employ to run their Lodge, a "High Performing" Lodge will prioritize Ritual, Education and Programing. The Past Masters should be

prepared to establish committees for each of these key areas. The IPM should advocate for these committees and see that appropriate resources are directed to them.

Committee Charter
A formal committee charter will define the purpose of the committee and ensure good governance, and desired outcomes. It will clearly establish its mission, delineate its resources and facilitate optimal communications among the stakeholders. Taking the time to prepare a charter will ensure the outcomes needed for a High Performing Lodge.

An Engaged and Motivated Past Master
One of the goals of this book is to provide the tools to motivate and encourage the Past Masters to stay active in their Lodge. In a very true sense, his path to the East was just a training ground for him to be an effective Past Master, a role he could nurture and develop throughout the balance of his Masonic career. He will come to see that the Past Master is an invaluable resource for a more active and high-performing Lodge.

Engaged and Motivated Cadre of Past Masters and Brethren
Each Past Master likely has his own passions, areas of experience and perspective on the Craft. It will be the responsibility of the IPM to recruit other Past Masters who may have drifted away and other Brethren from the Lodge to fill committees and implement the Worshipful Master's programs.

Community Outreach
The Past Masters should be in the position to promote involvement with the stake holders and influencers from within the community. By interfacing with the town council, chamber of commerce, police, fire or ambulance squads, the Lodge will be in a better position to participate in parades, fairs, celebrations and charitable events. Just as important as these groups are in helping us enjoy a meaningful relationship with the community, these are the very people who we want to attract to the Craft.

Assessed Gaps, Opportunities and Remedies
By using the tools discussed below, the incoming Worshipful Master will know what resources he has available to him and where these resources should be applied. By the time he introduces his program to the Lodge, there will be a great likelihood that his program for the year will be met with success. Successful outcomes are not the result of happenstance or luck, but rather the result of proper analysis and planning.

Lodge Performance Measures
By establishing Key Performance Indicators (KPI), the Lodge will be in a position to objectively measure its performance. Specifically, it will be able to collect and analyze data related to Lodge activity, which will identify where the Lodge may need to make some improvements. KPI related to attendance, membership or finances can, for example, help a Lodge make the right adjustments to keep the Lodge on track.

SWOT Analysis

By analyzing the current Strengths and Weaknesses of the Lodge in light of the Opportunities and Threats that exist outside of the Lodge, the Lodge officers can gain a common understanding or a true picture of the current state of affairs. After this analysis has been completed, any needed change or action can be applied. This quick and easy brainstorming technique can be done at any time to keep up with changing events.

SPOT Analysis

A SPOT analysis is an alternate brainstorming technique that can be used at any time to assess the current state of affairs and keep up with current events. Here we are assessing the Lodges Strengths and specific Problems in light of the Opportunities and Threats that may exist in the community or the society in general.

Project Management

Project management is a disciplined approach towards conducting any project that the Lodge or committee may undertake. It ensures that everyone involved understands the expected outcomes given the available time and resources committed to the project. Further, it will ensure that the project is being managed, and relevant milestones are reported as needed.

Guiding Building Principles for Role of Past Masters

- ✓ **The Past Masters Remain Subordinate to the Worshipful Master**
  In any case, the Worshipful Master has sole responsibility and authority to run his Lodge. Any assistance that is provided by the Past Masters must be done at the sole discretion and under the authority of the Worshipful Master. Any "Expert Authority" that a Past Master may have due to his tenure in the Craft is subordinate to the authority of the Worshipful Master.

  This should be considered as the PRIME DIRECTIVE or FIRST GENERAL ORDER of the Immediate Past Master. Elevation to the level of Immediate Past Master is not a second year in the East but an opportunity to share what you have learned with new Lodge leadership. It is the Worshipful Master who governs the Lodge.

- ✓ **All programs must maximize involvement of the Brethren**
  When every project, committee or event is run by the same individuals, others may feel overlooked or even shunned. These people are at risk of leaving. Masonry is about sharing everything. All planning should include an eye towards maximizing participation.

- ✓ **The Past Master must become acquainted with the concepts, responsibilities, and tools of his role.**
  The tools and resources necessary for the Past Master to operate an effective program are identified below. It should be the responsibility of the Past Masters to invest some time to acquaint himself with these resources and to use them, when fulfilling his role.

- ✓ **The Past Master should not burden the Worshipful Master with any additional responsibilities.**
  The Worshipful Master has his hands full conferring degrees, serving the Brethren and conducting the business of the Lodge. It is the role of the Past Masters to take some of the burden away from the Worshipful Master. To the extent possible, any project details or minor problems should be managed by the Past Master heading that committee.

- ✓ **As a Mason, the Past Master's conduct must be exemplary** (internally and externally).
  The Past Master will interface with new Masons, absentee Masons, other Past Masters, and members of the community; as such, his role will be very visible. For the sake of maintaining harmony among this divergent group of people, it is imperative that the Past Master maintains a reserved demeanor defaulting to the highest standards of Masonry.

Additional Thoughts

In years past, it was quite common for Lodges to have a committee of Past Masters, sometimes known as a Past Master's Association or a Permanent Committee. This body of experienced Masons would address any number of routine issues that would need constant attention, such as:

- ➢ To provide mentorship to current Lodge officers.
- ➢ To preserve the dignity, traditions, and teachings of Freemasonry.
- ➢ To assist the Lodge as needed.

A committee of Past Masters can be an invaluable asset to the Worshipful Master when unforeseen problems arise or if a complex issue needs to be unraveled and addressed. The Past Masters will be able to delve into the details and complexities of a sticky issue and come back to the Brethren with a workable solution ready for a vote.

When there are sufficient Past Masters available to form such a committee, it is advisable to use the Committee Charter format to capture the purpose and mission of the group.

CRITICAL TOOLS – SECTION II
Resource Modules 1 - 4

Resource Modules 1 - 4

Below are the resources available to the Past Master:

1. **Basic Facilitation Skills**

    a) **Listening Skills**

    b) **Promotion Skills**

2. **After Action Review**

3. **Masonic Motivation**

4. **More Active and Higher Performing Lodge**

    a) **Engaged Past Masters & Brethren**

    b) **Committee Charter**

    c) **Community Outreach**

Past Master's Framework (Part 1)

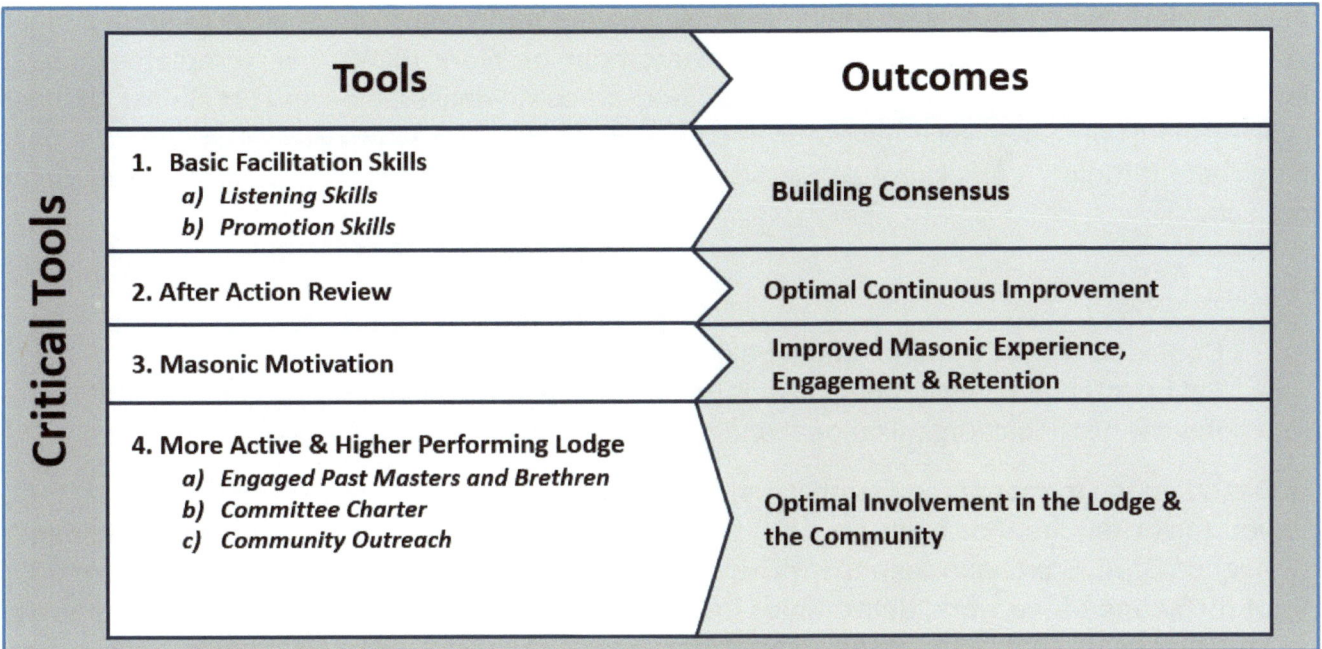

Module 1 - Basic Facilitation Skills

Introduction
Facilitation is the art of guiding a group to obtain consensus in areas of common interest through a collaborative and respectful environment. In other words, facilitation is the mechanism used by the leader to move a group to the fulfilment of its mission. This includes conducting meetings, seminars, focus groups, etc., to help them achieve their objectives. Training, Education, and Subject Orientation are all forms of facilitation. To give an example, during a meeting of the Lodge ritual committee, the goal might be to find ways to improve the quality of degree and other ritual work. As the meeting progresses through the facilitation process, ideas are generated, evaluated and then set forth for implementation.

The Process
As in any other professional practice, there needs to be diligent effort to use proven methodology and tools to ensure optimal results and outcomes. Facilitation has five steps or stages:

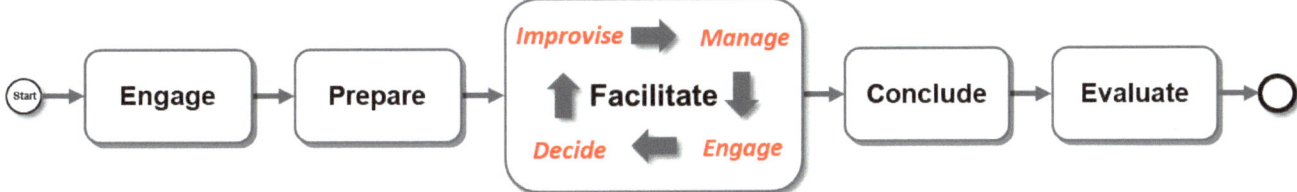

Engage

Understand the opportunity and decide how best to facilitate a project by considering the objectives, deliverables, stakeholders, roles, and constraints. Determine the format of meetings that you require e.g., in-person versus remote, Lodge room versus office or large versus small group. Before proceeding, put together a Statement of Work (SOW, see templates), i.e., a document that describes the scope of the project, expected deliverables and timelines. All those involved in this project must understand and agree to these parameters. A SOW is critical in case things get off target. A quick look at the SOW will keep the activity on track and the participants focused.

Prepare

> - Consider what information must be gathered or researched.
> - Set up interviews and gather information from relevant stakeholders.
> - Review historical, organizational and industry documents on the topic.

Based on the format of the meeting, determine how you will run each session and what tools you might require. For each session, prepare a Running Order Agenda and a Participant's Agenda Draft. Start each agenda with a summary of the SOW to ensure all parties are reminded of the scope of the work, deliverables and timelines. Keep the Worshipful Master informed and aware of your next steps. (Large and small organizations will benefit from proper preparation, which in this case would include a SOW and an agenda.)

Facilitate

Facilitate the meeting (with passion!). Manage the process, timing, and deliverables and decide if additional tools or adjustments to the process are needed. Continuously engage the participants. Throughout the process, continue to **Manage, Engage, Decide, and Improvise.**

> **Manage** - The facilitator is responsible for managing the process as outlined in the agenda. He is responsible for all the content being addressed and ensures that the participants meet the expected objectives and achieve the desired output and outcomes.
>
> **Engage** - The facilitator must involve **all participants** entirely in each step of the process. This includes drawing participants into the agenda topics and holding their attention. He must ensure that the energy level of the participants, both physical and mental, is maintained at all times. The facilitator needs to use a multitude of techniques such as icebreakers, exercises, team builders, and challengers, in addition to using stories, quotations and metaphors to make the topics relevant and interesting. As a facilitator one is in the "entertainment business."
>
> **Decide** - The decision-making process will typically remain in the hands of the facilitator in agreement with the sponsor. Whereas he may ask for the opinions of the participants, the final decision on agenda topics will be agreed to by the sponsor.
>
>> - In situations where the agreement of the participants is required, the decision may be made on a consensus basis.

> There are other situations where decisions are made based on weighted criteria, such as when purchasing technical products or services, where an agreed-upon criterion is used to evaluate the decision to be made.
> The question of "who decides" is generally agreed upon with the facilitator and the sponsor at an earlier stage.

Improvise - A facilitator must think through every step of the agenda items, considering numerous dynamics and situations, and improvise as required. For example, a facilitator may be using a technique to solve a problem and find that the method is not agreeable to the participants. At that moment the facilitator must quickly propose another option from his library of techniques to ensure the integrity of the process. Good facilitators always have backup techniques to switch to on short notice. One of the competencies of a facilitator is "Standing Alone." That means making a quick decision to keep the process going while gaining the group's confidence in the proposed approach or technique.

Thus, the cycle of the four factors —**Manage, Engage, Decide, and Improvise** —is executed in the session by the facilitator, much like a symphony conductor blending harmony while leading the ensemble and keeping an eye on every instrument.

Conclude

Once you have fulfilled all the deliverables as indicated in the SOW, it is time to prepare a report delineating the details of each one. Prepare a document that includes your conclusion, output, deliverables and next steps. Compiling this document is typically accomplished as a separate process, at the end of the project. Decide if you or the Worshipful Master will deliver this information to the Lodge or other stakeholders. Thank all who helped make the process successful. Even though the process is complete, once you have given this report, the following step is critical should a similar SOW be addressed in the future.

Evaluate

Evaluate the results and make recommendations for improving the process. Additionally, delineate any further opportunities that were identified, which could benefit the Lodge. Also, identify improvement opportunities for your own role/skills, and methods and tools. To be sure you have achieved as much as possible through this process, conduct an AAR as discussed in detail below.

Information Gathering to Action Plan

Through this process, the facilitator is essentially gathering information in order to devise an action plan. The following gives us an organized approach towards **information gathering, analysis, synthesis, and action plans.** A good way to start the process of information gathering is to use a technique called Brainstorming.

Brainstorming:

Brainstorming is a technique that helps groups generate large amounts of information about any topic of interest for the purpose of further analysis. It is typically followed by clustering the

information into meaningful themes or categories. Brainstorming is a group or individual creativity technique that is used to find solutions to specific problems by gathering a list of ideas that are spontaneously contributed by its member(s). There are four general rules of brainstorming:
- ➢ Focus on quantity of data.
- ➢ Withold criticism (no judging).
- ➢ Welcome unusual ideas (there is no bad idea).
- ➢ Combine and improve ideas (be innovative).

Affinity Analysis:
Now organize the various inputs according to related topics. This technique helps organize large amounts of data/information into manageable, understandable themes and is used in conjunction with brainstorming. It is typically followed by further analysis and actions.

Analysis and Actions:
After the brainstorming and affinity analysis, in this third stage, agreement is reached on the priority of these themes so that action can be taken to develop and implement solutions. The next step is to create an action plan or a formal project plan.

There are several ways to gather information and conduct analysis stated above. One is a simple template, and another is the use of sticky notes and flip charts and markers. How to design the workshop will be at the discretion of the facilitator.

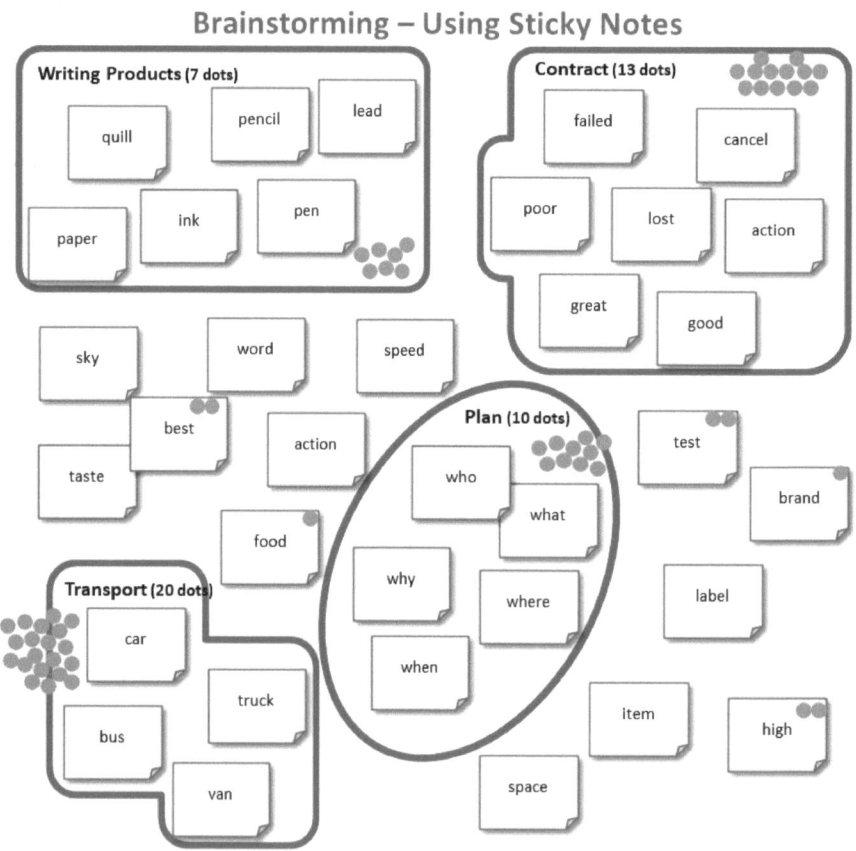
Brainstorming – Using Sticky Notes

Facilitation Template

Whereas, when there are a large number of participants, the use of sticky notes and a flipchart is desirable. Smaller groups may find it more manageable to use the Facilitation Template.

How to use the Facilitation template

1. Brainstorm ideas, issues, and opportunities in a meeting where Past Master (committee chair) or a designated Brother would jot down the information (be the scribe) or send out copies of the template to the participants to note their ideas, and then the Past Master would consolidate those in one single template. 2. Collaboratively discuss and cluster the information into themes or categories e.g., Lodge Building, Lodge Attendance, Outreach.

3. Mark these clusters into High, Medium, and Low priority. Create an informal action plan or a formal project plan.

4. The individual ideas which do not require funding or extensive research but can be fixed easily and provide value to the Lodge would be marked as Quick Wins (QW). Assign each QW to the Brethren for immediate action. This Continuous Improvement (CI) provides immediate benefit. For example, fixing the Temple door lock which sometimes does not work with the combination, thus making Brothers wait outside.

Facilitation Template

Lodge: Solomone Lodge No. 357	**Date:** June 24, 20XX
Purpose: To ensure that each new member develops competency in the symbols and allegory of each degree.	**Participants:** R.W. Arnold Sykes, PGC, W.B. Pete Smith, PM, W.B. David Jones, PM, W.B. Frank Finch, PM.
Facilitator: W.B. John Dokes, IPM	
Information	**Analysis**
Brainstorm Ideas: Provide handouts after each degree Prepare a Booklet for each candidate Have the candidates give a presentation Have the candidates write a paper Have the candidates meet regularly with a mentor Bring the candidate to other Lodges to witness degrees they just went through Bring the candidate into the Lodge on off hours to review the degree they have just experienced. Invite the candidate to ask questions in open Lodge, when the Lodge is open of the degree, they just experienced. Have the candidates sit with more experienced Brethren during collation Invite speakers to come to our Lodge to cover topics related to the degree work.	Themes/Categories: Literature (M) Provide handouts after each degree Prepare a Booklet for each candidate Candidate Involvement (H) Have the candidates give a presentation Have the candidates write a paper Invite the candidate to ask questions in open Lodge, when the Lodge is open of the degree, they just experienced. Mentoring (H) Have the candidates meet regularly with a mentor Bring the candidate into the Lodge on off hours to review the degree they just experienced. Travel (M) Bring the candidate to other Lodges to witness degrees they just went through Casual Learning (QW) Have the candidates sit with more experienced Brethren during collation External Resources (L) Invite speakers to come to our Lodge to cover topics related to the degree work.

Legend: Priority H (High), M (Medium), L (Low); QW (Quick Wins)

Agenda Design & Communication

There are two types of agendas: one for the participants and the second for the session leader. The session leader's agenda is called a Running Order Agenda (ROA) or Annotated Agenda. You first develop this ROA agenda and then finalize the participant's agenda.

Facilitator's Annotated Agenda (aka – Running Order Agenda)

Develop a detailed annotated agenda for facilitating the session. This includes topics, time, templates and materials needed. This agenda is a step-by-step detail of every aspect of the session to be conducted, both for training as well as facilitation. It is a script for the session leader of how the session would flow. This would be a design for the overall meeting but put together on an individual topic basis. This is time consuming but critical to gain confidence and envisioning success. This agenda is only for the session leader's use.

Agenda for Participants

Agree on the purpose, attendees, agenda, venue, and roles together with any relevant Lodge officers, who need to be involved. Outline session deliverables and agree on who will document the outputs and what tools are to be used. Also identify required facility needs e.g., room type, audio visual equipment, wall space, etc.

Resources and Facilitation Kit

Prepare your facilitation kit: projector, screen, any special charts, markers, paper rolls, masking tapes, note pads, pens, template copies, etc.

Communication

Before formal notice of the meeting, feel out what date and venue would be appealing to most of the stakeholders. Communicate the purpose of the meeting/session and venue to the participants. These can be the Lodge Brothers or outsiders depending upon the topic at hand. Plan the meeting and ensure refreshments etc., are arranged to make the session appealing and comfortable. In case the facilitator decides to send the facilitation, template and supporting material for the participants to complete, ensure it is sent with clear instructions.

Example of a Running Order Agenda

Lodge: Solomone Lodge No. 357	**Date:** June 24, 20XX
Purpose: Train the Mentor Workshop	**Participants:** Attach list names. **Facilitator:** R.W. Arnold Sykes, PGC, W.B. Pete Smith, PM, W.B. David Jones, PM, W.B. Frank Finch, PM See attached list of prospective mentors who are attending this workshop.
Facilitator: W.B. John Dokes, IPM	

A	Opening and Background - Review Agenda & Logistics; Ground Rules; Introductions Slide: 1 Dokes - Welcome Title Slide (Leave up during class gathering.) Slide: 2 Dokes - Ground Rules Slide: 3 Dokes - Agenda Slide: 4 Dokes - GL Mentoring Program Ask the participants to identify "what they hope to learn and expect from this workshop. Setup: a) Provide paper and markers around each table, and have the brothers discuss and jot down answers to the questions above. (Ask one volunteer on each table to be the scribe.) b) Give them about 10 minutes, and then have each table report out. c) Place the paper on the wall for visibility during the session.	9:00a 30 min.
B	Slide: 5 Sykes - Review some basic learning styles: visual-spatial: People who are strong in visual-spatial intelligence are good at visualizing things. These individuals are often good with directions as well as maps, charts, videos, and pictures. verbal-linguistic: People who are strong in linguistic-verbal intelligence are able to use words well, both when writing and speaking. These individuals are typically very good at writing stories, memorizing information, and reading. bodily-kinesthetic: Those who have high bodily-kinesthetic intelligence are said to be good at body movement, performing actions, and physical control. People who are strong in this area tend to have excellent hand-eye coordination and dexterity.	9:30a 30 min.
	Fast Forward Slides 6 through 77.	10:00 11:30
C	Slide 78 Finch – I Liked/I Wish Have the participants tell us what they liked about our workshop and what they would have liked to have seen done differently.	11:30a 15 min
D	Workshop Wrap-up	11:45a
E	No Slide Dokes – After Action Review With just the facilitators, discuss what went well and what needs improvement.	

Example of Participants' Agenda

Lodge: Solomone Lodge No. 357		**Date:** June 24, 20XX	
Purpose: Train the Mentor Workshop		**Participants:** List of Names of prospective mentors and guests, if any. **Facilitator:** R.W. Arnold Sykes, PGC, W.B. Pete Smith, PM, W.B. David Jones, PM, W.B. Frank Finch, PM	
Facilitator: W.B. John Dokes, IPM			
A	Sponsor Kickoff Review Agenda & Logistics; Ground Rules; Introductions		9:00a
B	Orientation of Learning Styles:		30 min.
	Fast Forward Slides 6 through 77.		90 min.
C	Conduct an After-Action Review to Gather Feedback for Continuous Improvement.		15 min
D	Wrap-up Workshop		11:45a

Note: In the participants' agenda, identify only start time, break time(s), and end time. For each activity provide an estimated time. This way, participants don't notice the clock-time changes in the time flow, giving the facilitator flexibility to adjust as needed.

Module 1a – Listening Skills

Introduction

The Facilitation process covered above is a useful tool that can be used to guide a committee towards the fulfilment of its mission. However, for it to be effective, the facilitator must get the most out of each member of the group; employing effective listening skills is therefore indispensable for the facilitator.

Up until now, you might have taken listening for granted. The fact of the matter is that even after having a detailed conversation, many of us will walk away with only a vague idea of what was said to us. To be effective in our communications, we must employ the proper listening technique to ensure that there are no misunderstandings or confusion.

Epictetus, the Greek sage, and philosopher (AD 55-135) stated: *Nature gave us one tongue and two ears so that we could hear twice as much as we speak.* The idea that we should be good listeners has a profound meaning for anyone in the role of a coach, mentor, facilitator, or leader.

The following seven foundational skills are essential for anyone in a leadership role.

- ✓ Active listening
- ✓ Questioning
- ✓ Information gathering and analysis.
- ✓ Public speaking
- ✓ Presenting
- ✓ Intervening
- ✓ Managing group dynamics

Active Listening is the most fundamental for an IPM or those in succession to become IPM someday. The following tool, i.e. the Listening Ladder, takes us through the steps of active listening; thereby, helping us become a good listener and an effective communicator.

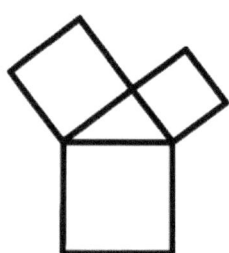

The Listening Ladder

Look	At the person speaking to you. Make eye contact to express that you are interested in what the other person has to say.
Ask	Questions. Ask follow-up open-ended questions to comprehend the meaning of what is being said by the speaker.
Don't	Interrupt or be interrupted. Ensure that the interruption is only for clarification of what has been said.
Don't	Change the subject. You will get an indication to change the topic when the speaker is finished with one thought. Look for cues to transition to another topic.
Empathize	With the speaker. Demonstrate this by a gesture such as "nodding your head" so that the speaker gets the message that you are interested in what is being said.
Respond	Verbally and nonverbally. Through body language such as nodding your head, eye/eyebrow movements, acknowledge that you are just as engaged in the conversation as the speaker is. You can do this without interrupting the speaker by saying, "…I see…" or "…I understand…"

The following is an example of the impression we make to people, when we are preoccupied or busy. It may seem extreme; however, when we have several things on our mind, this is exactly how we come across as people try to speak to us.

Without Active Listening	Speaker	Listener	Impression
Look	"Hello, how are you?"	No eye contact or looking around the room.	I'm being ignored, he's not interested in what I have to say.
Ask	"I'd like to give a short presentation in Lodge on James Anderson."	"Hmmm."	Wow, I guess this isn't a good idea, maybe I'll just drop the topic.
Don't	"Perhaps I can have a few minutes during…."	"Hey, come this way, I'd like to introduce you to…."	Boy, this is more complicated than I thought.
Don't	"Is there a time that works best for giving presentations?"	"The J.W. did a great job with dinner, don't you think?"	What?

Empathize	Seeking non-verbal clues.	Blank expression.	I'm not sure I'm getting through to this guy.
Respond	Seeking a personal connection.	Looking over the speaker's shoulder across the room.	He's not even paying attention to me.

If you are busy, preoccupied or for some other reason unable to listen intently, it is better that you find a time more suitable for a proper discussion. The speaker will truly appreciate a few uninterrupted minutes dedicated to him than a rushed and fruitless conversation.

With Active Listening	Speaker	Listener	Impression
Look	"Hello, how are you?"	Eye contact	It seems that I have his attention.
Ask	"I'd like to give a short presentation in Lodge on James Anderson."	"Oh, that's great, have you already prepared something?"	He seems interested. I'll tell him about all the work I did.
Don't	"Perhaps I can have a few minutes during our next meeting?"	"Sure, would you prefer to give the presentation in the Lodge room or downstairs during dinner?"	Great, he is giving me some options, he must be interested.
Don't	"Is there a time that works best for giving presentations?"	"I always want to support Brethren willing to give presentations, so, whatever works for you."	Wow, it seems like I'm in the driver's seat. I'm glad I made the offer.
Empathize	Seeking non-verbal clues.	Nodding in response to key points.	It seems I am holding his attention.
Respond	Seeking a personal connection.	Positive facial expressions and a few well-placed words.	Boy, this guy is really easy to talk to.

Obviously, this last example is preferable, since it employs all the lessons learned from the Listening Ladder. The speaker feels that the listener is fully engaged and truly interested.
For this to work routinely, you should continuously practice these techniques, whenever possible. In fact, try to practice this skill in your everyday conversations, both in your personal and professional life.

Additional Thoughts

There are certain instances where there could be tension or discord surrounding a particular topic. If this is the case, prior to proceeding to the *Listening Ladder*, it may be useful to start the listening process with a de-escalation step. Here we essentially invite the speaker to get it all off his chest and vent his concerns. As long as his comments remain relevant to the topic at hand, his input should be encouraged. Once the speaker has cleared his mind, he will be better able to move forward in a more focused and objective manner.

Module 1b – Promotion Skills

Why do you need promotion skills?

Learning how to promote concepts to the Brethren of your Lodge as well as to those of the community will enhance your ability to manage the variety of projects that you will be encountering as IPM.

- These skills will be useful in strengthening the relationship among the Lodge officers, the trustees, committees and the Brethren of the Lodge.
- You will learn how to present your case in an organized and cogent manner in order to achieve the goals of the Lodge.
- As you continue to interact with the Brethren and other stakeholders, they will gain confidence in your abilities.
- By learning how to best promote your Lodge within the District and the community, you will be able to differentiate the special qualities of your Lodge.
- These skills will help you put Freemasonry in the best light, when discussing its virtues with prospective members.

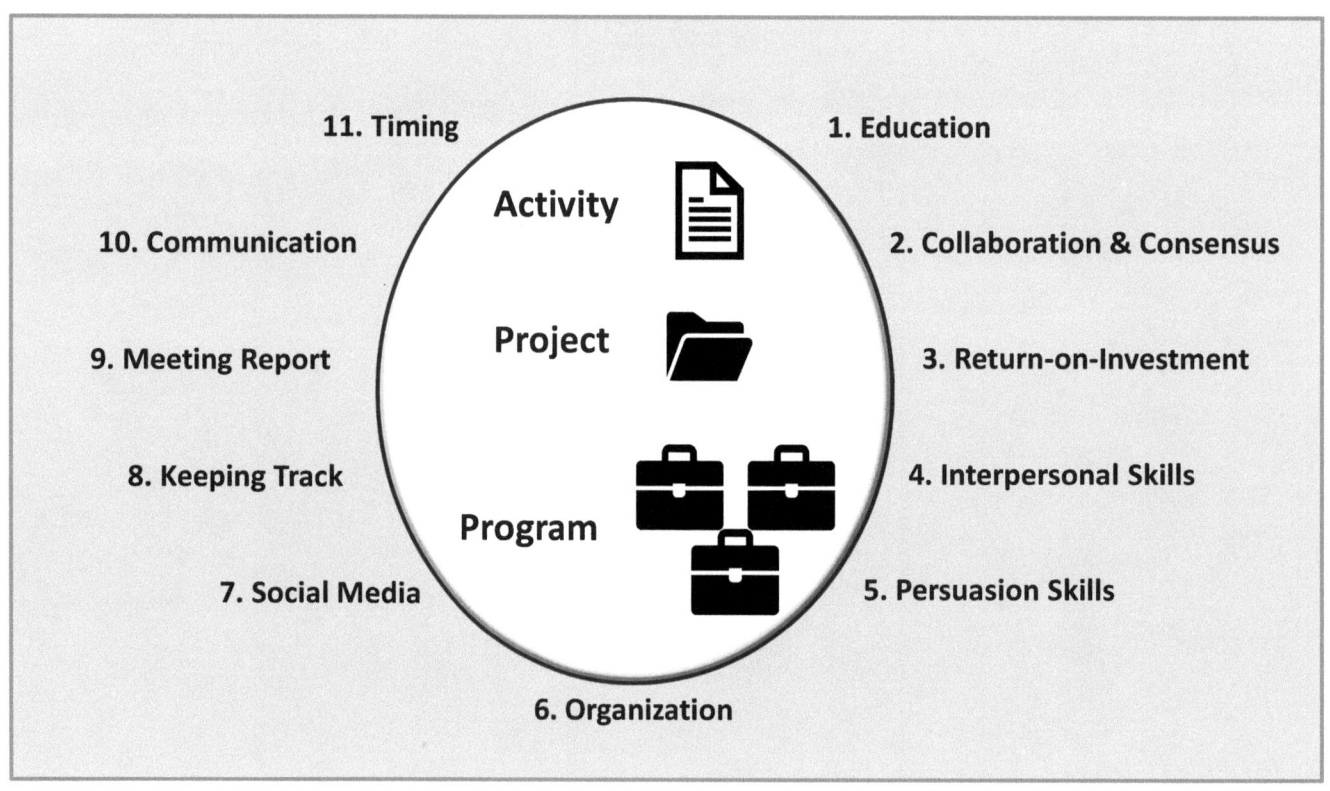

Essential Skills

1. Education
As the Immediate Past Master, you will be interfacing with new Masons, prospective members and members of the community. You will be their conduit to Freemasonry, and they will expect you to be able to answer their questions about the Craft. Although it is not realistic for you to answer every and any question, you should have a short-concise elevator speech prepared outlining the basics of the Craft. If a question that you cannot answer comes up from an important stakeholder, mayor, councilman, or police chief, be sure to return with one of your Lodge Brothers who can provide that information. (Remember, there is a lot of misinformation out there and we want everyone who works with us to be comfortable.)

2. Collaboration & Consensus
As a facilitator, committee chair or advocate, you will need to build consensus among various groups within the Lodge. Remember, the Lodge officers, the trustees, committees and the Brethren of the Lodge may each have their own goals, expectations and desires. Rather than overwhelming them with your ideas, programs and opinions, it's important to allow them to take part in the decision-making process and ensure they feel valued. Listen to their concerns and then augment your presentation so that it takes into account their perspective. This is called building a win-win scenario. (As previously discussed, it is imperative for the IPM to develop strong listening skills.)

3. Return-on-investment
Whether you are asking the Lodge for money for a project or asking the Brethren to invest their time, you must be prepared to explain what they will be getting out of this investment. This, of course, is critical when that investment is substantial or time consuming. A good way to demonstrate a return on investment is to show the Brethren the results of similar projects. For example, if you are planning a fund raiser, be prepared to discuss the return-on-investment that was enjoyed by the Lodge the last time they held such an event. Alternatively, you can point to the outcome of a similar event held by another Lodge.

4. Interpersonal skills
Anyone can develop interpersonal skills, and you don't have to be a "smooth talker" to develop good working relationships. Remember to be yourself and maintain a sincere approach in all your interactions. You can develop a better report with people by just following some of the following guidelines:

- **Greet everyone warmly.** Show people you are happy to see them and greet them with a smile and a handshake. (Think about how other people have made you feel welcome and important.)
- **Listen actively.** Listen to their needs and concerns and show that you understand them.
- **Use their name.** Using someone's name makes them feel valued and important.
- **Show empathy.** Show empathy by attempting to understand their point of view.
- **Be responsive.** If you need to get back to an individual, respond promptly to any inquiries or concerns.

> **Use positive language.** Use positive language to create a friendly and welcoming atmosphere.
> **Add value.** Think in terms of how your interaction has added value. How did your interaction address the needs of the individual with whom you just spoke?

5. Influencing skills
In spite of the fact that the IPM may have the best interest of the Lodge at heart, this may not necessarily be obvious to all the stakeholders. Therefore, it is imperative that the IPM be comfortable using persuasion to promote his concepts. Good persuasion skills will allow the IPM to demonstrate to the stakeholders why the ideas, programs and opinions are worth their investment. To persuade someone to your way of thinking, one needs to:

> Clearly understand the needs of the Lodge and demonstrate this to the stakeholders.
> Show how his ideas, programs and opinions are actually beneficial to the Lodge.
> Demonstrate to the Lodge officers, the trustees, committees and the Brethren of the Lodge that your goals are in line with their goals, expectations and desires. (You should feel that after you have spoken, you have just made someone's life a little easier.)

6. Organization
Understanding how the Lodge, District and Grand Lodge operates can help the IPM eliminate surprises and effectively manage various issues. Complete knowledge of the organization will enable you to anticipate the kinds of questions or concerns that might be raised by the stakeholders. Take some time to familiarize yourself with the budget, by-laws and committees of your Lodge as well as the Constitution and Laws of the Grand Lodge.

When working with your local government or other nonprofit organizations, be aware of their legal constraints or the ordinances under which they operate. By doing a little homework up front, you will be in a better position to build a strong and effective partnership with your neighbors.

7. Social media
Social media is a major way in which many people communicate today. Being familiar with how to use various media can give the IPM and edge in communicating with certain stakeholders. Whichever media you decide to use, it is critical that someone be in charge of routinely updating your social media presence, keeping your home page current with an up-to-date list of officers and all necessary contact information. Use your media presence exclusively for Lodge business, while maintaining an adherence to professional social media practices and protocols. Finally, be aware that not everyone uses the same social media platforms, to keep everyone in your Lodge informed, it may be necessary to use email, phone-trees or even the postal service to keep everyone informed.

8. Keeping track
Don't rely on your memory; get in the habit of carrying a bound notebook to jot down key information you may gather from your meetings and conversations. Alternately, keeping notes in your phone may be just as effective, just be sure to capture all significant information, as it comes to light. Remember that a brief, chance meeting in the hallway of a neighboring Lodge might be

just as important as a scheduled committee meeting in your Lodge building. The same holds true for a phone conversation or text message.

- In addition to a short note covering the topic of your discussion, record the date, location and name of the individual with whom you have spoken.
- Be sure to note any action items. If you promised to get back to someone, get back to him. You will lose the respect of people if you do not keep your promises.
- When you meet someone new, record their name & contact information. Even if you think you may never need to get in touch with them, there may be a time that it becomes critical that you reach them.

9. Meeting report

For planned meetings with key stakeholders or committees, be certain to record all the key topics from that meeting. Such a meeting report will likely follow the agenda and/or the Project Planning Template that should have been prepared in anticipation of the meeting.

A report intended to record the proceedings of a meeting held concerning an active project should cover the following points:

- Project Name or Description
- Context/Background
- Participants
- Achievements
- Obstacles
- Next Steps

Even if someone else is taking official minutes of the meeting, you need to have your own notes. Ensure that you have noted all action items to which you must respond and that you respond to all open questions expeditiously.

Remember: To be perceived as an effective pillar of the Lodge, you cannot necessarily rely on others to issue reports, minutes or action items. It is up to you to stay informed and respond to those who are awaiting your input.

10. Communication

Many of the elements covered in this training, such as listening, building empathy, analyzing and planning will be helpful in improving our communication skills. However, this section in particular covers some specific items, which should be followed to ensure your communication is effective. The following are the different kinds of communication, each of which has an important place in the communications spectrum.

> **A. Written communication:** Conveys information clearly, concisely, and with an accurate tone of voice. A well-written document is less likely to be misinterpreted and can be referred to regularly by all participants to refresh their understanding during the course of

a project. Any verbal communication which contains critical information should be followed up by a written communication.

B. Verbal communication: Is best used to convey complex concepts and to explain the intricacies of a project. Through verbal communication, we can receive real-time feedback, to determine if our message is getting across or whether you need to adjust your message to improve understanding.

C. Non-verbal communication: This includes body language, eye contact, and overall demeanor. We can cultivate strong non-verbal communication by using appropriate facial expressions, nodding, and making good eye contact. Verbal communication and body language must be in sync to convey a message clearly. This is an important part of face-to-face communication and is a particularly critical component of active listening.

D. Visual communication: This means using images, graphs, charts, and other non-written means to share information. Often, visuals may accompany a piece of writing or stand alone. In either case, it's a good idea to make sure your visuals are clear and strengthen what you're sharing. Do not overcomplicate your visuals and by no means, should they be allowed to distract from your message.

By the way: **When you receive a question, do the necessary research to give a full response. It is likely that the inquirer was looking for more than a short, off the top of your head answer.**

General: Whether verbal or written, email or Facebook post, in-person or virtual, communication must be viewed as a transaction. As with any transaction, it must include certain elements for it to be complete, anything less is counterproductive and demotivating. The following are important elements of any communication:

Be Concise: The IPM, *when acting as a facilitator*, is concerned about conveying information in a clear and concise manner. It is not time to tell stories or digress from your point. Instead of using long, detailed sentences, get in the habit of using short sentences, each containing one thought. Even when speaking, organize your thoughts in an outline of simple ideas that can be conveyed in a clear and organized manner.

Be Clear: All communications must convey an unambiguous thought or concept. Focus on the important issues and leave the details until everyone is clear on the concept. In written communication, use a reference line that conveys the main topic of the document. Use bold text to convey significant words or thoughts and arrange detailed thoughts using individual bullet points. Avoid the temptation to forward an old email to convey a new topic; this may confuse the issues. When starting a communication via email, start with a new template, type in a relevant title and ensure just the intended recipients are included in the email. Taking a moment to ensure intended recipients can certainly save a lot of miscommunication or unneeded explaining.

Be Complete: Give all the relevant information in your written communications. Don't assume that everyone knows the location of a particular meeting, just because it's "always there." New members to the group will feel left out or even shunned when this happens. Create a block of relevant information that is routinely used in your meeting announcements, i.e.:

Date:
Time:
Loc.:
Topic:
Contact:

Redundancy: In order to ensure that your target audience is processing your communications, it is sometimes expedient to present it in several different ways. This is especially true for complex concepts.

Additionally, when promoting an event, program or activity, an announcement should be sent as soon as the meeting is planned, a few days before the meeting and the day of the meeting. In cases where there may be months before the event, they should be sent out at regular intervals to keep the event fresh in everyone's mind.

For Video Conferences, a new invite should be sent out for each individual meeting. Don't expect everyone to dig out the last log-in coordinates.

Keep in mind that all our efforts to facilitate, organize and manage Lodge activity will be for naught, if we fail to communicate effectively.

11. Timing

One final note about timing. You must keep in mind that, if you are calling a meeting, it is imperative that you start that meeting on time. When others are waiting for the meeting facilitator to show up for a meeting that he has called, it shows contempt for the committee members and conveys a level of unprofessionalism.

The following is a brief example of how you might use Promotion Skills to sell the concept of a Festive Board to your Lodge or committee. Remember the amount of effort required in each area is dependent upon the level of understanding of your target audience.

Example

Promoting the idea of a Festive Board

1. Education – The first step is to educate the Brethren by actually defining a Festive Board; do not assume they know. A Festive Board can take many forms and should not be confused with a Table Lodge. Research the format you plan to employ and discuss it with the Brethren. (See "Developing a Culture of Enlightenment in the Lodge", Page #.) Don't forget to get input from other Past Masters in your Lodge or District, who may have experience in running a successful Festive Board. If you are successful in this first step, the following steps should go relatively smoothly. On the other hand, if you meet resistance, the educational process may need to be continued throughout the promotion process. Sometimes, you might need a "teachable moment" to get your point across. A teachable moment is actually an unplanned set of circumstances that may arise, providing you with an opportunity to convey a particular idea or concept.

2. Collaboration & Consensus – The only way you can move on to the process of actually planning a Festive Board, is to get the Brethren to be excited about it. Throughout the promotion process, your goal is to create true enthusiasm among the Brethren.

3. Return-on-investment – Everything worthwhile has a cost. For you to succeed, you must demonstrate that the benefit or return on the cost of a Festive Board is well worth the investment. The benefit in this case might be measured in terms of attendance, retention, enlightenment or other qualitative results.

4. Interpersonal skills – Whether you are addressing a group or speaking to an individual on a one-to-one basis, be sure to maintain a pleasing yet sincere demeanor. An important step in getting them to like the idea of a Festive Board is to get them to like you. After all, a Festive Board is mostly about Brotherly Love, the first tenet of Freemasonry. Everything related to the Festive Board should be enjoyable, even just talking about it.

5. Persuasion skills – As enjoyable as most Brethren find the Festive Board, there are always those who get stuck on the expense or some other concern. You need to understand that their concerns are legitimate and need to be addressed in a professional manner. Remember, if one stakeholder has an objection, there are likely others who have the same concern. Do not allow yourself to become frustrated but stay focused on the facts that you have gathered so far. Talk about the success of other Lodges, who have held a Festive Board as well as your projected return on investment. If you do not have good data to present, this means you need to go back and do some more homework.

6. Organization – Understand fully how a Festive Board might fit into the operations and culture of your Lodge. Are there Brethren within your Lodge, who might lead an academic discussion, present a paper or in some other manner arouse the intellectual curiosity of the Brethren? Is there sufficient budget to finance the festive board and does the Lodge have experience in organizing a well-planned dinner?

7. Social media – Social media is constantly evolving, so, it is critical that you use the medium most used by the Brethren. Don't forget old-fashioned emails, posters and even personal invitations. And don't forget the official method used by your Lodge to communicate, the Trestle Board and Lodge announcements. Whether you are still in the planning stage or sending out invitations, it is critical that you reach everyone in your intended audience.

8. Keeping track – There is a substantial gap between coming up with an idea and actually planning an event. Keep track of all objections and how you overcame them, keep track of all the volunteers and resources available to you. Remember to get in touch with those who are expecting your reply; for every promise you forget to keep or question that remains hanging, the less likely you will be able to succeed. The Festive Board has many moving parts. It may be best to use the Project Planning template (see Module 5d below) to keep track of everything.

9. Meeting report – It is important to keep notes of all meetings, whether they are short impromptu meetings or detailed, well-attended meetings. Never rely on your memory. Include the date time and venue of every meeting and list all those who were in attendance. List action items and those in charge of executing each action. Finally, continue to schedule meetings to assess your progress.

10. Communication – It is critical that before you hold your first meeting or send out emails and texts, you organize your thoughts in a written document for your own use. It should include all the elements found in the Education step, since you are likely going to need these data points in all your future communications. Include the definition of a Festive Board, the required investment of time resources and money, the projected outcome and who are the stakeholders, who needs to buy-in. Don't forget to give proper thought to those who need to be included in your communications.

11. Timing – Your first Festive Board will likely take time to get all the stakeholders on board and the resources allocated. Since it could take months, planning needs to start early. Once you get by-in from the stakeholders, you may need to form a committee to conduct the actual planning. Schedule meetings well in advance to ensure that all the participants will be able to add the date and time of the meeting to their calendar. Plan the date and time of the Festive Board on a date when most Brethren are available. Be sure to advertise the Festive Board months in advance to ensure optimal participation.

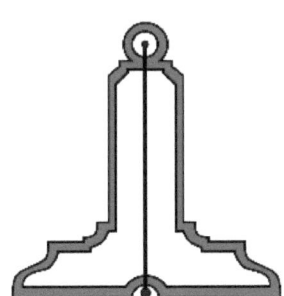

Module 2 – After Action Review

Introduction

"From the beginning of time, humans have survived and thrived by learning from their experiences, good or bad, and then improved their actions for better results next time. The catalyst for improving on their actions is the experience and knowledge of "what was" and "what could be possible." This knowledge, we apply moment to moment, activity to activity in our routine lives, both personally and professionally. This improvement approach happens unconsciously without giving much thought to our intent. However, if analysis is conscious and methodical with an eye towards continuous improvement, then next time around for similar situations the outcomes can be more rewarding and desirable."

After Action Review, Continuous Improvement Made Easy by Arjit Mahal.

After Action Review (AAR)

AAR is a technique of analyzing the results of any *Activity* by having the participant group members reflect on and acknowledge as to what was planned, what happened, and what could be improved next time around. This is a tool for continuous improvement (CI). An AAR can be conducted during the Activity or at its conclusion. An *Activity* in the context of Freemasonry may be defined as any action conducted by the Lodge such as committee meetings, social events, community projects or any other organized action.

In a Masonic Lodge there is always need for continuous improvement; in other words, an opportunity to conduct an AAR for degree work, Lodges of Instruction, fine-tuning Lodge protocols, installation ceremonies, official visits, festive boards, presentations, Lodge trips, maintenance projects, family events, festivals, parades and community events.

A Past Master in consultation with the Worshipful Master and other officers and stakeholders would conduct an AAR for <u>activities that matter most to a Lodge.</u>

AAR Facilitation

As in any other facilitation, brainstorming exercise, an AAR session should be planned in a safe congenial environment. If at all possible, an <u>AAR should be conducted immediately following an activity</u>, in order to assure quality input from the participants. There are two approaches to conducting an AAR, formal and informal. A formal AAR is meant for larger projects and may require time to plan and organize. An annual assessment of Lodge activity is an example of what might require a more formal approach to the AAR.

A more informal version can be conducted immediately following most of the routine activities of the Lodge. Depending upon the complexity of the activity under review, the scope of the process can be adjusted accordingly. We will discuss a more practical approach to the AAR process below.

There are three stages of facilitation.

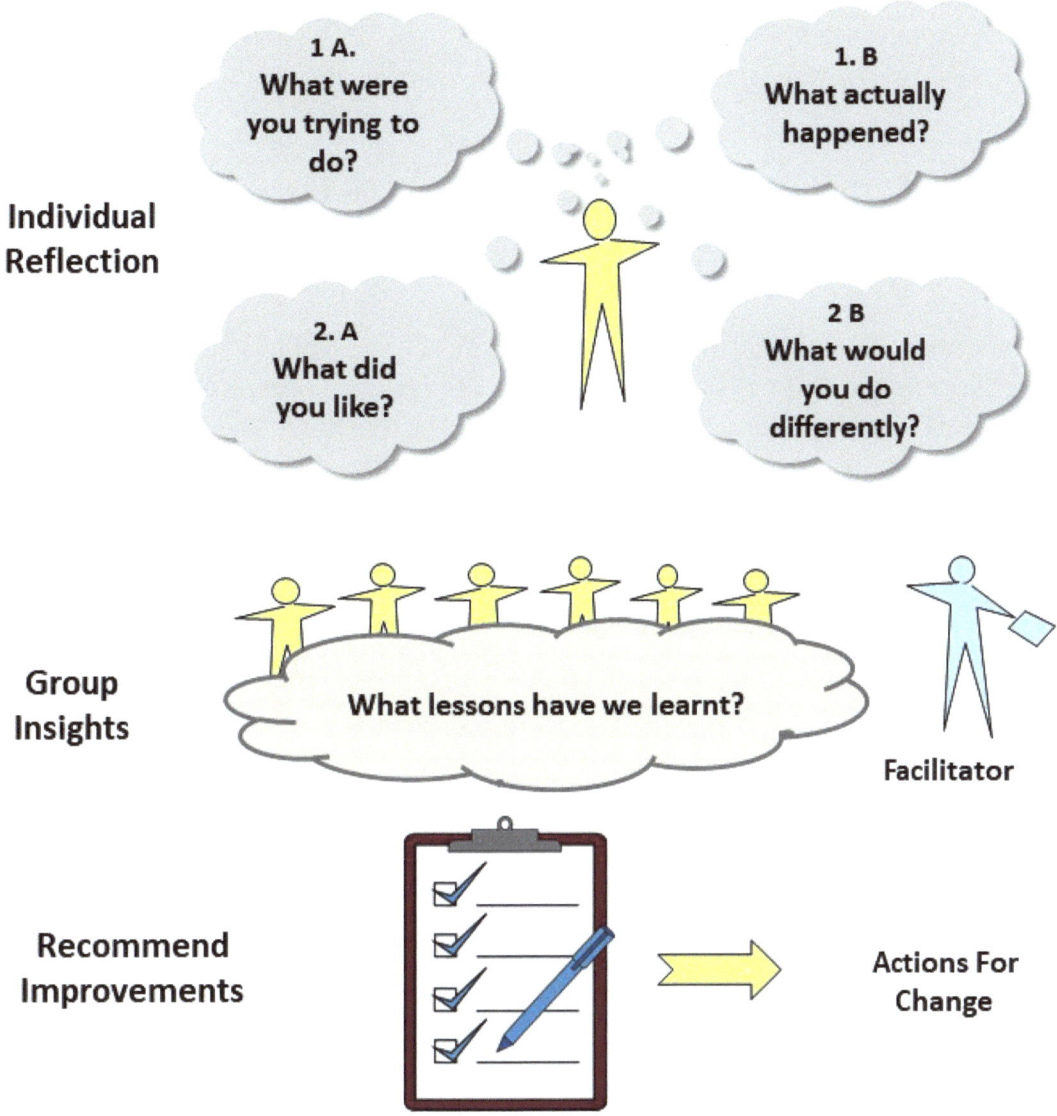

Stage 1 - Individual Reflections
The individuals directly involved in the activity are asked to think of these four questions below. This helps the individuals to frame their thoughts without any external influence.

- ➢ What were you trying to do?
- ➢ What actually happened?
- ➢ What did you like?
- ➢ What would you do differently?

Stage 2 - Group Insights
This is where all the participants and stakeholders of an activity collectively discuss the lessons learned, and frame ideas for improvement and change going forward.

Stage 3 - Recommend Improvements

From the lessons learned and ideas for the future, the whole group or an assigned subset would make a formal report and recommendation for change. This is generally where the AAR Process ends. As a rule, action items and specific changes to implement are not products of AAR. Some other projects may be kicked off to implement the ideas discussed and recommended in the AAR exercise.

An AAR can be conducted by the chairman of a committee following the fulfillment of their mission or project. The benefit of AAR is realized when the output of the **process** is shared with other teams and projects.

Additionally, the Lodge will benefit from an AAR at the conclusion of the Masonic year. A summary should be compiled by the **Past Master, Worshipful Master or Lodge officer** in charge of AAR and communicated to the incoming **Worshipful Master** and other stakeholders who can benefit from it. The timeliness of this communication is important because the participants want to see that the effort put into the AAR has been valued and benefits the organization overall as early as possible.

Further, since the incoming master has now participated in an After-Action Review, he should be able to repeat the process following his year as Master. By repeating this procedure each year as a Past Master, the Lodge is more likely to enjoy a higher level of success, while avoiding a repetition of problems.

AAR Facilitation Considerations and a Template

- Rules of Brainstorming encourage free thinking without judgement; don't limit quantity of input.
- "I Wish" term is important as it tends to stifle "finger pointing" towards any specific issue/Brother/team.
- It can be conducted in a short time ranging from 20 minutes to 45 minutes or less.
- Should not be conducted in a Lodge room but rather in another room with "intimate space".
- Instead of having a scribe jot down input from the Brethren on a template, the use of sticky notes applied to the wall or flip chart might be more effective. This will allow the input to be organized according to related topics as discussed above in the "Brainstorming" section. (While it may be tempting to use a computer to capture input from the Brethren, the use of old-fashioned sticky notes and a flip chart can provide needed flexibility for this process. Once the process has been completed, the use of a computer to document your results is certainly suitable.)
- Supplies Needed: Flipchart and markers (possibly sticky notes).

After Action Review

Topic & Scope:

Date & Venue:

Sponsor:

Participants:

Facilitator(s):

I Liked	I Wish

When finished, identify three to five top areas of improvement in the "I Wish" column with an Asterisk *. Assign someone to document the input collected.

Practical application of the After-Action Review:

Towards the end of his year as Worshipful Master, he should prepare himself for his role as IPM. This can be accomplished by first conducting an AAR of his year. He must dispassionately identify what worked, what didn't work and what resources were missing. He will then be in a position to identify possible solutions for any gaps that were identified.

Armed with the results of an AAR, the incoming IPM is now in a position to assist the new Worshipful Master in taking advantage of opportunities and recommendations for overcoming obstacles. At this point, the incoming Worshipful Master will be better able to form a successful program for his year.

By the time the incoming Master introduces his program to the Lodge, it should be ready for implementation. Moving forward, he will have a plan that includes the identification of committees to be formed, candidates for committee chairs, a staff to be recruited and resources to be allocated.

Further, through this process, the Master is able to present an optimistic vision for his year thereby encouraging the Brethren to attend Lodge and participate in a fulfilling program.

Additionally, since the incoming Master has now participated in an AAR through the efforts of the previous Master, he is now better prepared to conduct his own AAR towards the end of his year. By repeating this procedure each year, the Lodge is more likely to enjoy a higher level of success, while avoiding a repetition of typical problems.

Example of an After-Action Review

Venue: Solomone Lodge No. 357	Date: December 24, 20XX
Topic & Scope: To assess the activities of my year and to determine what should be added, dropped or improved upon	Participants: Worshipful Master & following Past Masters: W.B. John Dokes, IPM, R.W. Arnold Sykes, PGC, W.B. Pete Smith, PM, W.B. David Jones, PM, W.B. Frank Finch, PM
Facilitator: W.B. John Dokes, IPM	Sponsor: Paul Evens, Worshipful Master
I Liked	**I Wish**
We held all three degrees with our officers in our Lodge	I wish attendance was better during our regular communications
We had a nice family picnic during the summer	I wish we had more meaningful discussions during our dinner time
We had three speakers come to present at our Lodge	I wish we had more presentations from our own Brethren
The District Deputy visited our Lodge six times and seemed to enjoy himself	I wish our new Brethren were more active in the Lodge early on, they seem to look lost during our meetings
Most officers were in attendance at every meeting	I wish the older guys would attend our meetings on a more regular basis
There is always enough food and beverage at our collations	I wish we did a better job with our ritual and floor work

Recommend Improvements:

We should reprioritize our rehearsals and encourage attendance

Our collations should be in the form of a festive board with protocol and topics for discussion

The Brethren and candidates should give short educational presentations in Lodge

The Past Masters should act as mentors to the candidates and new Master Masons

Module 3 – Masonic Motivation

Introduction

In any organization, individuals, over time, can become less productive or lose interest in their area of work for various reasons ranging from apathy to boredom due to a lack of challenge, recognition of fulfillment. This may be referred to as "Burnout". The definition of Burnout is very broad; however, one simple dictionary definition of Burnout defines it as exhaustion of physical or emotional strength or motivation usually because of prolonged stress or frustration.

In the context of Freemasonry, we are using the term Burnout in the scope of the roles Masonic Brethren play in the functioning of a Lodge: when at some time in their Masonic career they may lose interest or motivation and then step aside from active involvement. This results in a Masonic "brain drain," which inevitably leads to a lack of support, leadership, mentorship, knowledge, and role-modeling, etc.

Variety – Adversity – Diversity – Intensity (VADI)

VADI is one leadership tool that can be used to assist the Lodge in assessing the memberships level of engagement at a time in point and then reinvigorating them to another level of desired engagement and thus "avoiding burnout." Following the VADI assessment, which identifies the current state of an individual's engagement, a brainstorming session can be conducted to identify a more challenging and engaging role that can be taken by a Brother.

To determine, if, a Lodge member may be vulnerable to "burnout," a self-assessment under the direction of a facilitator can be conducted using the following considerations:

- **V** - How **varied** have my experiences been to date?
- **A** - How much **adversity/challenge** did I have to face?
- **D** - How much **diversity** have I experienced?
- **I** - How much **intensity** have I experienced?

There are three stages of **Invigorating Masonic Motivation** for Brothers in a Lodge.

Stage 1: Conduct current state assessment of the Masonic engagement a Brother Mason has in his current role or situation—using VADI (as shown above).

Stage 2: If the current assessment shows that the engagement level is lacking in VADI having a lower score, then conduct brainstorming with the Brother to explore other options for inaugurating motivation. This could be utilized for active Brothers in the Lodge as well as for those whose attendance may have dropped, including the Past Masters.

Stage 3: Facilitate transition of the Brother to a more challenging or desirable role in the Lodge. This can be accomplished by a Past Master in collaboration with the Worshipful Master and other officers.

We know that the Immediate Past Master is sometimes the most vulnerable to "Burnout." It may therefore be expedient to routinely conduct an assessment as a Brother leaves the oriental chair. And, since we do not know the state of the Brethren in general, it is not a bad idea to conduct an assessment on a larger scale within the Lodge.

The following demonstrates how a Brother can conduct a self-assessment:

Stage 1: Audit your current Masonic history. In the current Role/Status column of the following template, have the Brother list all the duties and activities he has been involved with in the last year or two. In the last column, he can score his involvement on a scale of 1 to 10. 1 representing least enjoyable or challenging and 10 representing most intense and fulfilling. Add the total scores; low score is indicative of a Brother who may be close to burnout. While the scoring may be subjective, it would provide enough data to make a reasonable judgement of the cause of our lack of engagement in Masonic work/Lodge.

	Your Current Role/Status	1 – 10 (High)
V Variety		
A Adversity/Challenge		
D Diversity		
I Intensity/"Depth"		
	TOTAL	

Stage 2: Facilitate brainstorming by having the Brother come up with ideas and possibilities for improvement using this template.

Variety: Different chairs, committees, kitchen duty, visit Lodges, arrange socials, presentations

[ ]

Adversity/Challenge: Learn different rituals, working tools lectures, write a newsletter, help in trestle board writing, research Lodge history...

[ ]

Diversity: Visit other Lodges/Districts, socialize with Brethren of diverse backgrounds, take on building improvements, work for higher degrees...

[ ]

Intensity/" Depth": Masonic research and education, ritual instructor, mentoring ...

[ ]

Stage 3: Transition to a desired role or responsibility within the Lodge.

Consideration for Inactive Brothers

For Brethren who have become inactive, it may be useful to have someone conduct an assessment on their behalf using generally available information. Whereas such an assessment may not be precise, the Lodge can get a general idea of the motivation and level of engagement that a Brother or group of Brothers may have had in the Lodge. If it has been determined that the Variety – Adversity – Diversity – Intensity was at a low level, a Brainstorming session can be conducted to identify a means of improving the situation in the Lodge. It is more likely that Brethren will be motivated to return to the Lodge, once critical changes have been made to their possible role moving forward.

Additional Thoughts
Loss of participation is not just Burn-out. Predictable programs and events can get old. *(Consider a 3,5,7-year plan with something novel each year.)*

Example

Quality	Current Role/Status	Score
Variety	As a Past Master, this Brother is familiar with all three degrees and has been occasionally involved in helping out at rehearsals.	5
Adversity/ Challenge	He is not currently an officer in the Lodge and sits on the sidelines.	2
Diversity	He enjoys sitting with new Masons and candidates during collation.	4
Intensity/ Depth	He has committed many pieces of ritual to memory.	6
	Total	17

This Brother has scored 17 out of 40 in this assessment. This is not an extreme example given for dramatic purposes but is the current state of many Past Masters. He knows the work and is quite knowledgeable but is not being challenged. **We all want to be valued; what can we do with this Brother to get him more engaged and appreciated, while enjoying his Masonic experience.**

The results of a typical brainstorming exercise conducted with this experienced but underutilized Brother will identify roles that could be most interesting to him.

Variety: Committees, Community outreach, Events

Adversity/Challenge: Explaining the value of the Craft to the skeptical public.

Diversity: Dealing with the Town Council, Chamber of Commerce and various organizations.

Intensity/ Depth: Involvement with the town will require familiarization with various departments and policies.

Conclusion: This brother is ready to move beyond ritual and get involved in some of the more challenging roles of managing Lodge activities.

Apparently, although this Brother loves the Craft, he has outgrown some of the traditional roles offered within the Lodge. It appears that he would like to participate in planning events and activities that would involve the local community. This revelation might not have been uncovered, had he not gone through this self-assessment. Armed with this new perspective, this Past Master will be heading the Community Outreach committee, where he will be working with the Chamber of Commerce in the planning of parades, town picnics and other public activities.

Module 4 – More Active and Higher Performing Lodge

Introduction

An IPM with an understanding of basic facilitation skills, and armed with the results of an AAR, should now be able to put these skills and results to work. To form his committees and pursue the goals of the incoming Worshipful Master, it is first necessary to identify the Past Masters and Brethren of the Lodge, who will support these efforts. Obviously, the greater the resources, the greater the number of committees that can be formed and programs pursued. The following modules will help the IPM to motivate and engage the human resources of the Lodge, which he will need to fill committees.

Module 4a – Engaged Past Masters & Brethren

By the end of his year, the outgoing Worshipful Master should be prepared for his role as IPM. He should have the results of the VADI analysis of the Brethren putting him in a better position to identify those Past Masters, who are now ready for some challenging and rewarding work. It is important to get these Brethren involved as soon as possible in order to keep their positive momentum moving forward.

Once these reinvigorated Past Masters become acquainted with **facilitation and brainstorming skills**, they will be better enabled to lead a committee and support other Lodge activity. Now is the time to hold a Brainstorming session to identify the roles that these Past Masters can fill in order to advance the Worshipful Master's Program.

With the onset of the new Masonic year, the incoming Worshipful Master should be ready to implement his plan, and respond to the Lodge AAR, all with the support of the IPM, who should be ready to assemble the necessary committees. In very practical terms, this means getting a budget approved and Past Masters organized to head committees.

One of the most important functions of the IPM is to get all the members of the Lodge involved in some way to support the Worshipful Master's vision. Whether it is a sideliner, an absent Brother or dormant Past Master, getting these Brothers involved on a committee may be the most valuable assistance that the IPM can render.

It has been shown that when someone is made to feel appreciated or needed, he is more likely to stay active. Therefore, the IPM should keep an eye on attendance. After two or three absences, the IPM should contact the Brother and keep him abreast of the positive developments in the Lodge and see if that Brother might help out by participating on one of the "important" committees.

Each Past Master likely has his own passions, areas of experience and perspective on the Craft. It will be the responsibility of the IPM to match each Past Master with a committee, where his talents will be best utilized. The outcome of this process is twofold. First the Lodge will have a number of committees to address any number of opportunities and second, these Past Masters are given an important role, *i.e.,* a purpose for attending Lodge and participating.

Under the direction of the IPM, each committee head will be encouraged to recruit Brethren from the Lodge with the idea of involving as many as possible to achieve full involvement. It is at this point that the IPM will need to rely on all the skills discussed above, *i.e.* Listening, Promoting and Motivating. However, to properly charge all the new committees and keep track of their progress, it will be necessary to prepare a **charter** for each committee. This is covered in the next module.

Module 4b – Committee Charter

At the very least, a high-performing Lodge should include a Ritual Committee, Education Committee and a Programing Committee. We will discuss each of these committees in turn; however, we will start with the basic structure of a committee.

Introduction

The Masonic Lodges have permanent standing committees to govern the Lodge and its business, just as in any other non-profit organization. The Lodges typically have these committees: Finance, Blood Bank, Temple, etc. Then there can be *ad hoc* committees formed for some specific purpose and for a defined time frame with a clear set of guidelines.

Before a committee is formed, it is critical that the Lodge and its leadership fully understand its purpose; the preparation of a Committee Charter fulfills this requirement. A formal committee charter is a particular document that defines the purpose of the committee and other agreed details to ensure good governance, and desired outcomes. A Lodge committee would typically have Brother Masons as members but could include outsiders such as a contractor for the maintenance of the Temple. When a committee is formed, the Worshipful Master would typically encourage Lodge members to join, based on their interest or skill levels. (In order to facilitate efficiency and to avoid miscommunications, even smaller *ad hoc* committees need a charter.)

Charter
The charter may have several components, which include the following:

1. Purpose: This may also be called The Mission of a committee. This describes why the committee exists, what is the intent and, if applicable, how it aligns with the Bylaws of the Lodge. Example: *"The Student Scholarship Committee is charged with identifying three students annually from the high school to award Lodge sponsored scholarships"*. Be certain to decide if this is a **Standing, Permanent, or *ad hoc*** committee.

2. Authority: Describe who authorized the committee and reference the bylaws or guidelines of the Lodge or Grand Lodge that it follows. (This may be an optional clause).

3. Composition: Describe the names of the members and how they are selected. Depending upon the topic, select Brothers who have the right competence and motivation to serve and deliver the results.

4. Meetings: Describe the frequency of the meetings, both in person, or remote, such as phone or video.

5. Responsibilities: Describe the specific task the committee will carry out and what specific accountabilities the members will have. **See Exhibit A, RACI Matrix.**

6. Minutes and Reporting: The minutes must be documented and communicated to the Worshipful Master and the Lodge on agreed upon timeframes. A formal communication plan can be most useful to ensure that proper stakeholders are informed per the agreement. **See Exhibit B, Communication Plan.**

7. Termination: Describe when the committee would have fulfilled its mission and would be honorably closed. At the conclusion, conduct an After-Action Review. Thank all those who participated and contributed.

RACI Responsibility Matrix. Exhibit A.

R - Responsible	Name the "Doers" here
A - Accountable	Has Veto power – There can be only one name here e.g., Worshipful Master
C - Consulted	Consult and have two-way communication
I - Informed	Inform after decision; one-way communication

Communication Plan. Exhibit B.

Stakeholder	Message	Frequency	Mechanism	Who	When

Example of Charter format

Name of Committee: Mentoring Committee	Type of Committee: Standing	Date formed or authorized: June 24, 20XX
Purpose of Committee: To ensure that each new member develops a competency in the symbols and allegory of each degree. The committee will recruit and assign mentors as needed.		
Authority: The Lodge voted on June 24, 2025 to form a Mentoring committee.		
Composition: The Committee will be made up of at least five Past Masters and any of the knowledgeable members who may be motivated to participate.		
Meetings: The committee will meet from 6:00 to 7:30 p.m. at the Lodge on rehearsal nights.		

R - Responsible	W.B. John Dokes, IPM, (Chairman) R.W. Arnold Sykes, PGC, W.B. Pete Smith, PM, W.B. David Jones, PM, W.B. Frank Finch, PM.
A - Accountable	The Worshipful Master
C - Consulted	The Worshipful Master and the Sr. Warden
I - Informed	Progress reported once a month to the Lodge on meeting nights.

Stakeholder	Message	Frequency	Mechanism	Who	When
W.M.	Progress Report	Twice a month	email	W.B. Dokes	After each meeting of the committee.
S.W.	Candidate Status	Once a month	email	R.W. Sykes	Beginning of each month.
Lodge	Status Report	Once a month	verbal	W.B. Dokes	At the first Lodge meeting of the month.

Termination:
This committee will continue to operate indefinitely or unless disbanded by vote of the Lodge.

Examples of committees that exist in most high-performing Lodges.

Lodge Ritual Committee: Everything that is of value to us as Masons springs from our ritual. A well-run Lodge should aspire to confer all three degrees with its own resources. To achieve this goal, planning over a series of years is required. Each Brother's level of competency in the ritual should be monitored. Armed with this information, the committee can endeavor to encourage specific Brethren to advance their competency in the ritual and provide them with opportunities for training and rehearsals.

Lodge Education Committee: As mentioned above, everything that is of value to us as Masons has its roots in our ritual. To ensure that we all understand the allegory and symbolism of our ritual, some effort needs to be invested in educating the Brethren in these matters. Whether it is the Grand Lodge Mentoring Program or some other program, there needs to be regular sessions offered by the Lodge to impart Masonic Light. To advance this effort it is necessary to recruit instructors and mentors from within the body of the Lodge.

Lodge Programing Committee: To stimulate attendance and inspire the Brethren, entertaining and informative programs are an indispensable part of every Masonic communication.

1. There are many sources that can be tapped for Lodge programs; however, before going outside your Lodge look within.

   A. As part of a candidate's education, you might want to encourage him to report to the Lodge on some of the aspects of the allegory or symbolism of his recent degree.

   B. Find someone in your Lodge who might want to report on his Masonic travels or experiences.

2. Your Grand Lodge may maintain a list of speakers who will be willing to travel to your Lodge.

3. Most Lodges have a Library which can be used to prepare presentations or support Lodge discussions.

4. Typically, civic, community and business leaders will be more than willing to speak at your Lodge.

5. Police, Fire or Ambulance Squads can give demonstrations and discuss their role in the community. (This can be part of your community outreach program.)

6. Monitor programs within the District & State and organize car-pools for visitations.

For any committee to perform effectively, it needs to have some basic performance standards (**See Module 5a**). The IPM and the Committee Chairs need to be in a position to monitor the activities of each committee to see that they are on track to achieve their goals. If things go off-track, it is better to find this out early so that corrective action can be taken.

Module 4c – Community Outreach

Introduction

Whereas the Brethren and Past Masters of the Lodge will be directly responsible for managing their committees, the IPM will have one committee that he should head himself, *i.e.* the Community Outreach Committee. It is only through community involvement that the average person will be able to experience what Freemasonry brings to the world. Further, getting involved in the community is something that will pay the Lodge back in many ways. As a trained facilitator, communicator and committee organizer, the IPM will be prepared to interface with both external organizations and those relevant committees already operating within the Lodge. He should be prepared to address the following questions:

1. Is the Lodge involved in community events such as parades, fairs and celebrations?

2. Does the Lodge promote its events to the town council, chamber of commerce, police, fire or ambulance squads? Does the Lodge participate in theirs?

3. Are there shelters, food drives or other charitable activities that the Lodge could support?

4. Are local youth sports teams supported?

5. Is there some equipment needed by the police, fire or ambulance squads?

6. Does the Scholarship Committee's mission need to be updated or expanded? Is the Lodge membership sufficiently involved? Are the scholarship recipients honored at a special meeting?

Additional Thoughts

We must keep in mind that charity and community involvement is not a matter of writing a check or buying a ticket. It means personal involvement.

Public Relations: Any community involvement or charitable activity should be reported to the local media outlets. Advertising our activity allows the community to see what we do.

TOOLS to Use Anytime – SECTION III
Resource Module 5

Resource Module 5

Below is an additional resource available to the Past Master:

5. Assessed Gaps, Opportunities and Remedies

   a) Lodge Performance Measures

   b) SWOT Analysis

   c) SPOT Analysis

   d) Project Management

Past Master's Framework (Part 2)

	Tools	Outcomes

General Tools (Use Anytime)	5. Assessed Gaps, Opportunities & Remedies
	   a) *Lodge Performance Measures*
	   b) *SWOT Analysis*
	   c) *SPOT Analysis*
	   d) *Project Management*
		Viable Programs for the Success of the Lodge

Module 5 - Assessed Gaps, Opportunities, and Remedies

Introduction

The topics covered in this module provide the out-going Worshipful Master with additional tools that can be employed along with an After Action Review to assess his year. As discussed above in **Module 2**, the soon-to-be IPM, having conducted an AAR of his year, will be better able to discuss possible gaps, opportunities and challenges for the incoming Master to consider. So that, when the incoming Master introduces his program to the Lodge, it will have taken into account the assessment conducted by the previous Master.

With a well-thought-out program ready to launch, the IPM can now assist the new Worshipful Master by forming committees required to execute the program. It is now time to prepare committee charters (**See Module 4b**), allocate resources and recruit committee chairs. However, once the committees are formed and funded, the IPM must be prepared to assess their progress and keep them on track. This can be accomplished by establishing Key Performance Indicators, (KPIs), following a Project Management protocol and conducting SWOT or SPOT analyses as outlined in this module.

Any gaps, which are identified through a SWOT or SPOT analysis, can be characterized as a missing resource. For example, a gap analysis could identify that there needs to be additional Brethren recruited for a particular committee, financial resources may need to be approved to fulfill a committee's goal or a particular Past Master with a specialized skill needs to be persuaded to join a particular committee.

As the year unfolds, the IPM needs to anticipate that problems and obstacles, as well as new opportunities, may arise. It is critical that he be prepared to identify these challenges and know how to adjust the Worshipful Master's programs accordingly. More specifically, the dynamics within each committee need to be monitored to ensure that its intended goals will be met. Once these remedies or solutions are organized and prioritized, the members of the committee need to be aligned with a course adjustment.

In order for the IPM to make best use of his time, he should encourage the committee chairs to become acquainted with the pertinent skills covered in this book. This will enable them to be in a better position to conduct analyses and management processes on their own. With its members becoming acquainted with these processes, these committees will become more effective over time.

As the Worshipful Master approaches the end of his year, and in preparing himself for his role as IPM, an AAR of his year should be conducted. This allows the incoming Worshipful Master to have the same beneficial information starting his year as was available to his predecessor.

Whereas, this section is useful to manage committees or assist a Worshipful Master in planning his year, it should be remembered that these skills can be employed at any time.

There is no committee too small or Lodge activity too minor that will not benefit from these tools.

Additional Thoughts

In the course of monitoring the effectiveness of the committees, the IPM should keep his fingers on the pulse of the Lodge. No matter how ambitious or well-designed the Lodge programs are, it is critical to stay in touch with the morale of the Brethren. This is probably the most important gap analysis that an IPM can conduct.

Module 5a – Lodge Performance Measures

Performance Measures: The art of establishing measures includes the understanding of "what matters most" and then collecting the data to determine gaps. For example, one measure can be Lodge attendance against paid membership. This may be considered a **KPI – Key Performance Indicator.**

Introduction

Performance Measurement is the process of collecting, analyzing, understanding, and reporting information regarding the performance of a group or an organization, with the aim of ensuring sustainability and desired progress.

In order to measure performance, one must first establish Key Performance Indicators, (KPIs), which is a quantifiable indicator of progress. A KPI for a Lodge could be Lodge attendance, the number of degrees a Lodge conferred or the number of events the Lodge may have sponsored. Each of these KPIs is easily identifiable and easy to measure. The more KPIs that are identified and measured, the more likely a Lodge will be able to effectively measure its progress. However, to keep the process manageable, at least the most critical KPIs should be monitored.

Lodge Performance Measures

At a minimum, there are some basic areas where each Lodge should focus, *i.e.*:

Area	KPIs
(1) Membership	Active, dues paying, withdrawn, etc.
(2) Structure	Health of the line, succession planning, competency
(3) Operations	Meetings, speakers, education, travel, charity, community events
(4) Finances	Income, expenses, assets, debt and physical structure
(5) Future Planning	Immediate and long term

The KPI examples given above are quantitative. In other words, they typically measure only the numbers associated with each KPI. Below are examples of specific *quantitative* questions that are easily answered by reviewing attendance records, trestle boards, committee reports and Lodge minutes. By answering these questions, a Lodge can get a good start on assessing the performance of the Lodge.

Meetings
    On average, how many members attend a typical Lodge meeting?
    On average, how many VISITING Brethren did you have at a typical meeting?
    How many educational presentations did you have this past year?

Events
    Does your Lodge offer social events for the Brethren, how many?
    Does your Lodge hold social functions that include family, how many?

Education
    How many Masonic educational events were held last year?

How many Masonic educational events did your members travel to last year?

Does each EA, FC and new MM have an ASSIGNED mentor(s); how many mentors have been assigned?

Travel
How many times have your elected officers travelled to other Lodges?
How many members attended District or Grand Lodge events?
How many members attended the annual Grand Lodge Communication?

Charity
How much money did you give to non-Masonic (*i.e.*, the community) charities last year?
How much money did your Lodge donate last year to Masonic entities?
How much money did you donate to Brethren (or their families) in need?

Community events
How many community events did your Lodge participate in?
How many attendees did you have at the last open house?
Did you award a 'First Responder of the Year' this past year? How many attended the ceremony?

Lodge Finances
How much money does your Lodge have (total)?
How much money did your Lodge collect in dues this past year?
Did your Lodge rent out its facilities? What were the revenues?
How much money did your Lodge raise this past year in fund-raisers?
Were you within budget for this past year? What was the over/under amount?

Lodge Planning
Did you have a program scheduled for each Lodge meeting for the year? How many in total?
How many rehearsals do you have per year?
How many Past Masters are in your elected line (not incl Treasurer / Secretary)?
How many Past Masters are in your appointed line?

Once you have taken stock of the *quantitative* data for the base year, it will be relatively easy to compare it to subsequent years. The numbers for the new year will either be higher or lower than previous years and therefor the areas that require improvement will be immediately evident. Concurrently, where numbers improve, you will see where the Lodge has strengths.

Methodologies for Performance Measurement
Whereas a quantitative analysis of Lodge KPI's is a good start, there is really much more that needs to be accomplished in order to assess the Lodge performance; therefore, a more *qualitative* assessment needs to be undertaken.

If we continue with the earlier examples, we would need to measure not just the numbers, but other parameters such as the <u>success</u>, <u>effectiveness</u>, <u>competency</u> or <u>levels of enjoyment</u>

associated with Lodge attendance, the degree work and events. Whereas, quantitative results are easily obtained, qualitative results require more detailed analysis by using questions, surveys and interviews. In any case, both quantitative and qualitative analysis must be used when measuring performance.

Lodge Performance Measurement Process (a qualitative approach):
First create a Standing Committee for Lodge Performance Measurement. Establish a charter with appropriate membership on the committee with a chairperson in charge. The committee needs to brainstorm and determine the most critical qualitative KPIs. The next step is to prepare a list of open-ended questions geared to get feedback from the Brethren or other relevant parties.

Answers to these questions should then undergo an affinity analysis, in the same manner as is done in any brainstorming exercise. By organizing the answers according to related topics, the divergent answers will soon make sense, and the important inferences will rise to the top.

Lodge's Strategic Plan. Simply put, identify long-term and short-term objectives of the Lodge. This can be done by brainstorming or conducting a SWOT analysis (**See Module 5b**). The "weaknesses and threats" provide clues to what needs attention, and which KPI data show that the Lodge is moving in the right direction.

- ☐ Next identify KPIs, which matter most, and send a Survey Questionnaire to the membership (initially select fewer measures that can be managed accurately).

- ☐ Once you have gathered responses to these questions, it is time to analyze this information and determine how the Lodge will improve its performance.

- ☐ Implement improvements and plan to measure additional KPIs for the following year.

Qualitative data can also be obtained with an AAR as alluded to in Module 2. It is advisable to get in the habit of performing an AAR following every Masonic event sponsored by your Lodge, while the experience is fresh in everyone's mind. You can conduct a simple *I Liked - I Wish* questionnaire or a more detailed survey with questions specific to the event. In either case, you will have valuable data to assess the effectiveness of the event.

The following is an example of a short survey that you might use to assess three key performance indicators. You can conduct this survey as a group activity or hand out surveys to individuals, who can return the survey at some future point. In any case, it is not necessary, nor is it a good idea to request the names of the respondents.

Comment on your general impression of our Lodge meetings.

I Liked	I Wish
Everyone seems to know his part; the opening and closings tend to run smoothly.	I wish we didn't spend so much time debating every detail relating to the bills.
We usually open Lodge on time with everyone in their seats.	I wish we had a regular time during our meetings for presentations or discussions.
During the business section of our meetings, everything is fully explained.	I wish we could keep certain past masters from talking to each other during our meetings.
Most meetings are kept to 90 minutes.	I wish we could have more members coming out to our meetings.
The Worshipful Master uses his gavel to keep things moving along.	I wish the Brethren would learn to wear the correct apron in Lodge.

Comment on your general impression of our degree work.

I Liked	I Wish
We typically confer three degrees during the year.	I wish we didn't rely on other Lodges to fill-in with lectures and other parts.
I like that Brother Jones is always there to do the Middle Chamber lecture.	I wish that each officer would know his part before taking his chair.
I like that Brother Jones is always available after the FC degree to discuss the symbolism of the degree.	I wish we had more Brethren available to mentor our candidates.
We typically have all the officer chairs filled at each degree.	I wish we had more candidates for each degree.
I like the organ music that we have during each degree.	I wish we weren't always hunting for the working tools and other props before each degree.

Comment on your general impression of our collations.

I Liked	I Wish
I like the pizza we usually get for our collations.	I wish we had a quality dinner with white tablecloths, something to look forward to.
I like that collations are short, so I can get home early.	I wish we used the collation as an opportunity to discuss Masonic concepts.
I like the free drinks we get at collation.	I wish more Brethren would stick around following our meetings to enjoy Lodge fellowship.
I like that there are always leftovers to take home at the end of the night.	I wish we had more guests from the community joining our collations.
I like talking to the Brethren about their family and work life during our collations.	I wish the stewards were actually helping with the preparation of the Lodge collation.

Module 5b - SWOT Analysis

SWOT Analysis: This assessment technique can be used at any time to understand the current state of an area of interest and then determine what action needs to be taken. Armed with the results of an After-Action Review and a SWOT analysis, the IPM can effectively identify opportunities and make good recommendations for overcoming obstacles for a committee, the Lodge or even small projects.

Overview: Any organization, for profit or non-profit, from time to time, must take a checkpoint to determine the "health" of their organization to ensure that it cannot only survive and sustain itself but also can thrive under changing circumstances.

Since the Masonic Lodge is also an organizational entity, it too has similar needs. The "health" of a Lodge can be measured from many points of view such as ritual competence, conducting degrees, attracting new initiates, financial viability, facilities management etc. A SWOT analysis is a means of assessing the ability of a Lodge or committee to continue in the fulfillment of its mission.

SWOT (Strength, Weaknesses, Opportunities, and Threats)
In a simple SWOT analysis, a group brainstorming exercise is conducted with relevant stakeholders around the four quadrants as shown in the template **below**. As they provide their input, each comment is assigned to one of the quadrants. Similar ideas are then clustered and summarized via an *affinity analysis*. At this point, a number of actual strengths, weaknesses, opportunities, and threats should have been clearly identified.

The SWOT analysis will allow the officers, Brethren and other relevant stakeholders to gain a common understanding of the current state of the Lodge. This analysis actually provides input for determining the need for any change or action that must be taken.

This activity can be conducted on a small scale, as in the case of a committee or on a large scale as in the case that involves the entire Lodge. **As alluded to earlier, it is recommended that an incoming Worshipful Master request a SWOT analysis prior to his term, so that important improvements can be instituted during his year and beyond.**

Template Explanation: <u>The Strengths and Weaknesses are generally internal; Threats and Opportunities are generally external to the organization</u>. Strengths and Opportunities need to be leveraged more, whereas weaknesses must be converted into strengths. The threats are the constraints that must be managed/minimized and/or converted into strengths.

Note: *In some cases where an organizational entity may have many known problems, instead of SWOT Analysis, SPOT Analysis,* (**See Module 5c**) *can be done the same way. SPOT: Strengths, Problems, Opportunities and Threats.*

STRENGHTS (Leverage)	WEAKNESSES (Convert into Strengths & Opportunities)
THREATS (Minimize & Convert into Opportunities)	OPPORTUNITIES (Leverage)

Facilitation Process

1. Identify/determine and agree on the **scope** of the area to be analyzed (a committee, Lodge activity, officer duties, or any other area, which matters most at a given point in time).

2. Identify a list of participants (stakeholders) and establish a venue: date, time, and location. Arrange for food and beverages to ensure the participants are comfortable during this exercise. The room must have a large wall space to put large sheets of paper using painter's tape.

3. Create a SWOT template on a wall-chart; this entails preparing an area designated for assembling inputs under the heading of either Strength, Weakness, Opportunity or Threat. Provide large or medium-size sticky notes (4 in x 6 in) along with appropriate markers. Explain the concept of SWOT, its purpose and the expected outcomes to all present. Instruct them to write one idea per sticky note and write yet another note below the idea on the same sticky note. This would explain the consequence of the item for clarity. An item above the line and the implication below the line in the following figure.

ITEM
Implication / Consequences

4. Once an individual has created a SWOT item, he should then place it on a common wall chart for group analysis. (As in any brainstorming exercise the more ideas the better.)

5. Now cluster the sticky notes into themes and prioritize for further action. Document the output and determine next steps of action/project planning. As appropriate, share the results with the Lodge membership.

Supplies: Large sheets of facilitation paper, markers, painter's tape, flip chart with stand.

Example of SWOT Items with Implications Notes

Strengths	Weaknesses
ITEM	**ITEM**
The officers are proficient in conducting all three degrees independent of any external help.	The annual revenue stream of the Lodge is less than the total expenses (by $5,000 approximately).
Implication	**Implication**
The Lodge excels in ritual and degree work and can offer help to sister Lodges in the district, as and when needed.	Lodge cannot sustain itself in the long term. Lodge is not able to organize interesting programs for the membership.
Priority: M	*Priority:* H

Opportunities	Threats
ITEM	**ITEM**
There is a request from sister Lodges inside and outside of the XYZ Masonic District to provide some officers for degree work in support of the gap in their line of officers.	The new Masons initiated into the Lodge do not understand the Masonic/Lodge protocols and conventions.
Implication	**Implication**
Our officers can gain more experience while helping sister Lodges. It will promote cross-pollination of Masonic knowledge among Brethren and enhance networking.	If not corrected, this may inculcate behaviors not consistent with Masonry.
Priority: M	*Priority:* H

Module 5c - SPOT Analysis

SPOT (Strengths, Problems, Opportunities, and Threats)

SPOT Analysis may be facilitated just as shown in the SWOT template; however, in this case the headings are Strength, Problem, Opportunity or Threat. The SPOT template shown below is an alternative approach for gathering brainstorming data.

How to decide SWOT vs. SPOT Analysis:
For gap analysis for any entity or area of concern, generally SWOT analysis would be the best start. However, if it is known that there are serious problems to be resolved and threats to be managed, and the stakeholders' concerns are high, SPOT analysis may be more appropriate. Among the cross-functional stakeholders, sometimes the term "problems" may be contentious due to politics and turf considerations. In that case, the Sponsor (The Worshipful Master) of the analysis initiative and the Facilitator must determine the best option.

Facilitate these four areas: The Greatest Strengths and Serious Problems are generally internal; Serious Threats and Greatest Opportunities are generally external to the area of focus. Below is an example of the kinds of input that might be gathered during a SPOT Analysis.

Example of SPOT Analysis

(See appendix for a blank SPOT Analysis template.)

SPOT (Strength, Problems, Opportunities, and Threats)

SPOT Analysis may be facilitated just as shown in SWOT template. This template is an alternative approach for gathering brainstorming data. (Note: SPOT Analysis may be conducted when the problems are serious and need attention relatively soon.)

Greatest Strengths (Typically internal to the Area of Focus):
1. *Officers are proficient in ritual and degree work, w/o external help.*

2. *Updated kitchen with nice meals offered during collation.*

3. *The Lodge is known in the community for its scholarship program.*

Serious Problems (Typically internal to the Area of Focus):
1. *There have been no new members in two years.*

2. *Experienced Brethren and Past Masters seem to be drifting away.*

3. _Lodge income is dwindling due to loss of dues income._

Greatest Opportunities (Typically external to the Area of Focus):
1. _Sister Lodges are requesting the Lodge's assistance with ritual work._
2. _Community requests our involvement in upcoming parade._
3. _A sister Lodge has asked to collaborate with us on a fund raiser._

Serious Threats (Typically external to the Area of Focus):
1. _Newer members are not competent in management or business skills._
2. _The average community member has strange ideas about Freemasonry._
3. _Other fraternal organizations are also having difficulty raising members._

Module 5d – Project Management

Introduction

A project is a temporary endeavor undertaken to create products, or services or bring about some change in organizational processes, roles, technology, or infrastructure.

In the case of a Lodge, project examples include renovation of the Temple building, participating in the Founder's Day Parade or organizing a holiday event for the Masonic families.

How can a Lodge benefit from a methodical approach to project management?

- ✓ Improve stakeholders' satisfaction by understanding their expectations and meeting their needs appropriately. (The stakeholders include Brothers and non-Masons.)
- ✓ Decrease costs by optimizing use of resources including time, money, personnel, equipment etc.
- ✓ Gain better control over project's progress and manage risk more effectively.

Balancing Triple Constraint: Quality/Scope, Time, and Resources. If scope is bigger, more time and resources are needed. If there is less time, then the scope must be reduced, and resources increased. If resources are short, time and scope need to be reduced. *(Source: "To Do Doing Done!", G. Lynne Snead & Joyce Wycoff)*

Project Planning Steps

Any project can be easily managed, if, we take a few minutes and proceed with an organized approach towards devising a plan. Just by following these steps, you will have all the information at hand to ensure that expectations and resources are properly managed.

Project Vision: Understand the purpose of the project, i.e., the benefit that the stakeholders would receive resulting from the project. *"What are the expected results of this project and what is the added value to the Lodge."*

1. **Project Description -** *"Describe the objective of the project, and what is in scope and that what is out of scope."*

2. **Deliverables -** *Identify major deliverables: tangible outputs and outcomes expected to be delivered*

3. **Cost, Budget & CSFs -** *Identify cost and assumptions, and Critical Success Factors*

4. **Risk Management -** *What may be the risks and what is the plan to mitigate those*

5. **Launch Project: See Project Planning Template (next page).**

6. **Close Project:** Report to the Lodge, Conduct After Action Review, and archive project artifacts/papers etc.

Roles and Responsibilities

Sponsor	**This is likely the Worshipful Master of the Lodge.** Makes commitment of resources on behalf of the business and is the conscious of the project ("signs the check").
Champion	**This could be the Wardens, or Treasurer.** Ensures the delivery and acceptance of project results. Removes any roadblocks.
Project Manager	**This could be an IPM or any Brother with the competence to manage the project.** Plans and manages the day-to-day activities of the project. Motivates the team, communicates with the stakeholders. Manages risk. ("on the line")
Team Members	Dedicated to conducting the day-to-day assigned activities.

Advisory Group	Provide specialized knowledge and perspective.	
Others	May include internal or external service providers for specialized work.	

Note: These skills are fundamental to the Project Management process, which entails delegating work, gaining agreement, collaborating, and effectively communicating with all stakeholders.

Example of Project Plan Initiation

Project Plan Initiation

1 – **Project Name:** Festive Board (F.B.)	2 - **Program Name:** Enhancing Lodge Activity

3 - Description/Context: It was determined by the W.M. and a committee of Past Masters that by offering a well-planned F.B. on a regular basis, the Lodge would enjoy the following results: Improved Attendance, Candidate and New Mason Involvement, Opportunities for Discussion and Dialog Among the Brethren on Masonic topics and an Exciting Venue for Visiting Brethren.

4 - Scope/Deliverables: The goal is to develop a protocol for holding a well-planned F.B. following one meeting per month. We will also need to prepare a budget for the menu and speakers.	**5 – Organization/Communication Plan**: We will poll the Brethren to assess, menu ideas, topics for discussion, who might want to make a presentation then prepare a recommendation for the W.M.

6 – Approach: A F.B. is intended to be an enjoyable and fulfilling experience for the Brethren; therefore, we will endeavor to get as much input from the Brethren as possible, while keeping them informed of our progress.

7 – Assumptions and Constraints: We suspect that the cost of a menu for the F.B. will be higher than the cost to the Lodge for a typical collation, we will endeavor to identify economies.

8 – Financials: On average, the Lodge pays $300 per collation only receiving $120 in donations; therefore, the net cost to the Lodge is $180. We will try to stay close to these figures when preparing a budget.

9 - Mile Stones:

#	Activity/Deliverable	When	Who	Status
1.	Introduced Basic idea for the F.B.	13JANXX	W.M.	Ok'd
2.	Discussed the advantages of a F.B.	27JANXX	Brethren	Introduced
3.	Secured the commitment to prepare a menu.	10FEBXX	Stewards	Committed
4.	Secured the commitment to help cook, set up and serve the food.	24FEBXX	Volunteers	Committed

| 5. | Discussed the economics of a F.B. | 24FEBXX | W.M. | Agreed |
| 6. | Received Lodge approval to finance the F.B. | 10MARXX | Lodge | Pos - Vote |

10 – Close/Learnings:

When the F.B. concept was properly explained to the Brethren, the Stewards and two

volunteers agreed to purchase and prepare the food. The projected price of the F.B.

menu will be in line with our typical collation cost, which relies on catered or take-out food.

Further, with improved attendance anticipated, donations are expected to be higher,

and surplus funds will be earmarked for an occasional Masonic Speaker.

Conclusion/Summary/Next Steps

If you are seeing these tools for the first time, you might not feel comfortable using them right away; this is quite understandable. What you should do, in any case, is try some of them out; like anything else, as you start using them, you will become used to them and eventually come to rely on them.

Imagine yourself the head of a committee answering questions from the Brethren of the Lodge during a stated communication. You're standing all alone, maybe sweating a little bit and you get barraged with "well, what's wrong," "what are you doing about it," "who's in charge," "who's on the committee with you," "when will you have something concrete to report" and "how much is this costing the Lodge?" The tools presented in this book will allow you to answer all of these questions calmly and with authority. You can leave the meeting with the confidence that you have given the Brethren a competent response to all of their concerns. Without the judicious use of these tools, the result of this routine meeting could have been disastrous. So, for the sake of your "future you," you can start by picking one of these modules and make it your own.

Although, it might seem overly simple at first, the art of listening must be learned and practiced. This might be one of the first modules that you should take to heart. If we go back to the Lodge room, where you are being hit with a number of tough questions. The "Listening Ladder'" will be a life saver. By making eye contact, the Brother knows that you are actually paying attention. By letting him finish his remarks without interruption, he's made his point, got it all off his chest and is now ready to hear a response. By asking open-ended questions of the Brother in order to help him clarify his position, you are showing your empathy and willingness to speak with him further. Finally, by using the appropriate body language, you can communicate a sympathetic demeanor.

What you have just done is help the Brother make his point clearly, while minimizing any risk to the harmony of the Lodge. As you continue to practice the use of the "Listening Ladder," you will notice that your communications will become more fruitful and more even-tempered.

If we return to the above example, where you are being barraged with questions at a Lodge meeting, your best friend will be the "Committee Charter." You'll have most of the answers you will require all there in black & white. The <u>Purpose</u> of the committee will lay out exactly why the committee was formed and what problem, concern or task it will address. It will say by what authority it was formed, it could be the by-laws, or it could be the Worshipful Master. There will be no question as to why the committee was formed. It will list all who are members, when they meet, the responsibilities of each member and key stakeholders. Finally, it defines when the mission of the committee will conclude.

Armed with the "Listening Ladder" and a "Committee Charter," you have taken the first steps towards becoming a credible committee chairman. However, to actually run a committee, you will need to become comfortable with <u>Basic Facilitation Skills</u>.

Probably the most important thing to remember relative to facilitating a meeting is that it should **start with an agenda** and **end with an action plan**. If you remember this, you will be ahead of most business professionals. As chairman of a committee, you know that it is critical to prepare an agenda in advance of addressing its members; however, you should consider preparing an agenda, whenever you plan on addressing any group. This will ensure that you get your message across, convey all the relevant information and keep yourself and your audience on track.

However, it must be kept in mind that an agenda is not just an outline of things that you want to discuss, but it is actually the product of your research into the details of your scope of work. Once your initial research is complete and an agenda prepared, only then are you in a position to have a meaningful dialog with your committee or stakeholders. If someone approaches you informally to ask you a question about the committee, it is acceptable to say you'll get back to him once you get some additional input. It is better that you delay a couple of days rather than convey half-baked or unverified information.

Finally, once you start using the facilitation process, you will become comfortable and at ease, when it comes to managing complex issues with a variety of potential outcomes. The process allows you to take what seem at first like weird and crazy ideas and arrange them into a cogent and manageable plan of action.

So, in the end, we recommend that you become comfortable with these tools, so, you can make your Lodge become a perpetual source of Brotherly Love, Relief and Truth.

ADDED VALUE – SECTION IV

Although, the above five training modules were covered independently; in practice, many of them will be implemented concurrently. In other words, it takes a number of different skills to manage a Lodge and to achieve its goals. The following examples will show how certain outcomes can be achieved by implementing the skills you have learned.

General areas where the IPM/PM can help the Worshipful Master and the Lodge

1. What is the mood of the Lodge, does the Worshipful Master need to step in to preserve the harmony?

2. Does the Worshipful Master need help in composing his Trestle Board?

    A. Does he have an inspiring message?
    B. Are the various committees providing sufficient input?
    C. Does the Lodge have updated information on Grand Lodge and District activities?

3. Is everything conducted in accordance with the *Constitutions and Laws* of the Grand Lodge?

4. Are the Treasurer and Secretary working well together and are all fiduciary standards being met?

5. Masonic Communication is the core of the Masonic experience and proper attention should be given to planning and execution. Where can you help?

    A. Is there a schedule of speakers or programs for the Worshipful Master's year?
    B. Is the Jr. Warden doing an effective job in arranging for an enjoyable collation?
    C. Do those responsible know how to properly set up the Lodge room?
    D. Is there someone responsible for ensuring that all the Brethren are in their seats before the sound of the gavel?

6. In case the Worshipful Master is under pressure or distracted, are visitors being properly welcomed? Does the Sr. Deacon understand his responsibility to, "introduce and accommodate visiting Brethren?"

7. Is the Lodge prepared to confer all the degrees? Is there a Lecture you can learn or part you can take to fill in the gaps? Do you need to help a Brother with his part? Do you need to step in and encourage the Brethren to attend rehearsals?

8. Is anyone paying attention to those Brethren, who have been missing Lodge meetings?

9. Is there someone organizing attendance for District events, installations, official visits and receptions? Remember, the Secretary's job is to maintain lists, send out correspondence and

issue reports. It is really up to the Worshipful Master and the IPM to actually motivate and encourage the Brethren to represent the Lodge at various Masonic events.

10. Is there someone regularly in touch with the other Lodges of the District?

11. Who from your Lodge is attending Grand Lodge? Who needs motivation? Who needs help?

Additional Thoughts

Leadership in Lodge Meetings: Quality leadership requires planning, organization and punctuality. The IPM should discuss the format of the agenda he used during his year. What pitfalls did he find in running a meeting and what worked well? If during a meeting, the Worshipful Master finds himself embroiled in a run-away discussion, the IPM might recommend that the topic be tabled, and a committee appointed to consider the topic.

Friendly Meetings with the IPM: The Worshipful Master and the IPM should meet regularly on an informal basis to share ideas. They should work together to discuss programs, committees and problems. It is likely that the IPM will have already addressed some of the problems now faced by the Worshipful Master.

Developing a Culture of Enlightenment in the Lodge

If you are lucky enough to travel to other Lodges and Jurisdictions, you will surely notice that there are Lodges that have discovered the path to a successful and enlightened Lodge. You should keep in mind that developing a culture of enlightenment in your Lodge is within the grasp of any group of Masons. The key is to pursue the individual passions of those who make up your Lodge. As long as you attempt to pursue a balance of Brotherly Love, Relief and Truth, *i.e.* the three tenets of Freemasonry, you cannot fail.

The 1st step is to develop your resources. These resources will provide you with the magic of Freemasonry and inspire you to apply its principles and learn its lessons. Here are some basic resources that can make a quantum change in your Lodge:

- Library
- Discussion Groups
- Lodge Presentations
- Forums & Societies
- Travel

As you go through building your resources, think about what you are passionate about and what you would like to take on as a project. Don't put all the pressure on your W.M. or S.W., think about the added value that ***you*** can bring to the Lodge.

Although most Lodge libraries already have at least a few books of consequence, there are always new books coming along that are worth your attention. Rather than relying on the Lodge to buy new books, it is suggested that each member finds a book that intrigues him and then donate it to the Lodge Library after he has read it. In this way, the approval of Lodge funds does not need to be an obstacle to your building a library.

It is likely that there will be someone in your Lodge with the motivation to act as the Lodge librarian. If you do it right, the awarding of this responsibility will be seen as recognition or even a reward for services rendered. He can draw up a list of books, note who donated which books and who may have borrowed a book.

Just a few of the books to consider for your Library:

- *Encyclopedia of Freemasonry* by Albert Mackey
- *Introduction to Freemasonry* by Carl H. Claudy
- *American Freemasons*, by Mark A. Tabbert
- *Better Angels of our Nature* by Michael A. Halleran
- *Masonic Jurisprudence by* Roscoe Pound
- *Illustrations of Masonry* by William Preston
- *Constitutions of 1723 & 1738* by James Anderson
- *The Old Charges of the Craft* by Guy Chassagnard
- *The Spirit of Masonry* by William Hutchinson

It is an unfortunate reality that unless we are encouraged to actually read these books, most of us would be content to stack them in a well-finished oak bookcase and let them gather dust. It is therefore recommended that someone take charge of organizing a book club, where an assigned book can be discussed at an informal meeting of the Brethren. Alternately, there can be a time allocated at every communication to have one Brother report on a book with discussion to follow.

If you are successful in establishing a book club, you will see that it will soon morph into a discussion group. The topics broached by the assigned book will inevitably give rise to questions and debate. With this in mind, all the Brethren should be encouraged to attend the meeting of the book club, even if they haven't read the book.

When you are back in Lodge, be sure to give a short report on what went on at the book club meeting; more people will attend, once they discover how much fun you are having. Don't forget the Trestle Board, let the Lodge know the date and time of your meetings, so they can make time in their calendars.

By the way, a book such as the *Encyclopedia of Freemasonry* by Albert Mackey is one that needs to be accessed on a regular basis as candidates and inquiring Masons endeavor to seek the answers to any sort of question. Mackey's book is available on *PDF* and can be downloaded by every brother of the Lodge, essentially giving every Brother access to many of the most puzzling questions that we as Masons may face.

When planning for speakers to be invited to your Lodge, we sometimes overlook some of the most knowledgeable and motivated speakers available to us. These are our candidates and new Master

Masons. Remember, they have just made a major decision to dedicate their lives to learning and self-improvement. Give them an opportunity to share some of the excitement they are experiencing. They can discuss topics related to their degrees or symbols and allegory taken from the ritual. Certainly, a Past Master or another venerable member of the Lodge will likely have a paper up his sleeve, if you just ask. In any case, you need to look internally before you look for visiting speakers.

Someone on the education committee can be in charge of connecting with any number of Masonic forums and societies that are out there. Most have a publication that can be the source for Lodge presentations and even visits to symposia that they might sponsor. The following are some of the most popular:

- Philalethes Society-*The Journal of Masonic Research*
- Masonic Society-*The Journal*
- Quatuor Coronati Lodge No. 2076-*Ars Quatuor Coronetorum*

For those who are seeking something special, the magic of Freemasonry is found in travel. When travelling to visit Lodges or Masonic events in other Districts, Jurisdictions or countries, you might be surprised at how, in spite of slight differences in ritual, we all share the same values and follow similar paths. On the other hand, seeing how things are done in other Lodges, might give you the inspiration to try something new and exciting.

Remember, Masons, who you meet for the first time, are not strangers, they are friends, who you have never met before. Therefore, you should not hesitate and squeeze in a visit to another Lodge, whenever possible. Rather than waiting for an opportunity to present itself, it would be more expeditious to recruit a committee chair, who has either the experience or passion for travel.

To start with, there are Lodges in your District or Jurisdiction that are conferring degrees or sponsoring a speaker. They will most likely be thrilled to accommodate your visit. The Travel Committee chair would then establish a travel group from among the Brethren and set up carpools. Use your Trestle Board to announce your travel plans. Of course, you should contact the host Lodge, society or event chair, to let them know you are coming. If you are planning to attend a formal Masonic communication or degree, it may be necessary to have someone there who can vouch for you. Alternately, you may need some extra time to prove yourself a Master Mason. If you are travelling to a Lodge outside your Jurisdiction, it may be necessary for you to get permission from your Grand Secretary, who might need to contact the host Grand Lodge on your behalf. In any case, Lodges are always expecting visitors, and you shouldn't feel uncomfortable about visiting another Lodge.

Following each excursion, it is critical that you share some of the highlights of your visit with the Brethren of the Lodge. Let them know that additional Masonic enlightenment is just over the horizon and that they should consider joining you on your next visit abroad.

As an easy first-step, establish a routine of visiting neighboring Lodges in your District. Your Travel Committee chair can read their Trestle Boards and announce to the Lodge, degrees, speakers, table Lodges and fundraisers planned nearby. If you make the effort to support their Masonic activities, they will likely reciprocate. Don't forget, a personal invitation to the Worshipful Masters in your area will go a long way in strengthening fraternal bonds. Some Lodges have established a Lodge uniform or a custom Lodge tie; this will make your Lodge members easily identified in a neighboring Lodge or venue. One last thing, rather than relying on an old worn-out apron that a host Lodge has been lending to visitors for decades, invest in a white leathern apron reflecting personal pride, while also reflecting well on your Lodge.

Lodge Presentations

In anticipation of his year in the East, the Senior Warden can prepare a tentative schedule of topics to present at each meeting. Once the topic has been identified, the next step is to find a Brother who will do it justice. Remember, *Mackey's Encyclopedia of Freemasonry* is an invaluable tool capable of supporting any Brother in the preparation of a short presentation. The following is a list of interesting topics that correspond to the season:

Season	Topics
1st meeting of the new year.	The Obligations of a Freemason.

(Some Lodges have a rededication, where the obligations of and E.A., F.C. & M.M. are repeated.)

Mid-winter	The Baltimore Convention of 1843
G.W.'s Birthday: Feb. 22, 1732,	George Washington
End-winter	Symbols & Allegories of the 3rd°.
Spring begins	The Hiramic Legion.
Tax Season	Ancient Myths & Freemasonry.
Grand Lodge Communication	The Constitution and Laws reviewed.
Mother's Day	Jephtha

(Following his victory over the Ammonites, Jephtha would wind up sacrificing his daughter to G-d.)

Memorial Day	Masonry transcending war.

(Read and discuss - Better Angels of our Nature by Michael A. Halleran)

School year is ending.	The *Age of Reason* & Freemasonry.
Feast of John the Baptist, June 24th	John the Baptist
Labor Day	Masonic Bible Verses Dissected
Fall begins	The Landmarks of Masonry
Fall	Symbols & Allegories of the 1st°.
Harvest Season	The wages of a Fellow Craft
Election Day	Masonic Statesmen
Thanksgiving	Table Lodge & Festive Boards
Winter	The "Middle Chamber Lecture".

Without venturing too far from the resources held by every Lodge, it should be possible for candidates and new Masons to easily prepare presentations for the Lodge. Remember that the ritual itself has numerous clues designed to develop the mind and heart of a Mason. To start with, young Masons should be encouraged to explore the symbols and allegory found in the degrees.

This review, in most cases, is quite necessary since the candidate may have missed the significance of elements within the degree as he quickly went through the experience. In fact, most Masons will need to witness a degree many times, before fully appreciating the messages being conveyed throughout a degree.

One significant yet often overlooked part of the first degree is the *Rite of Destitution*. This lesson in charity can be explored from different angles and in his presentation the Entered Apprentice Mason can give examples of when he may have relied on the charity of others or has himself bestowed charity. Even more basic, this is a good opportunity to explore the definition of charity. Since charity is such an important element of Freemasonry, it may be a question continually asked and answered throughout one's Masonic career.

Besides the ritual itself, the Volume of Sacred Law (VSL) is part of the furniture of the Lodge and is therefore accessible to every Mason. As our rule and guide for our faith and practice, the Brethren should be encouraged to explore it as a resource and not merely to be revered as a sacred object. Most Lodges in the English-speaking world will have the King James Version of the Bible on its altar. In as much as, many of the lessons found in this bible are secular in nature, Masons should not feel they will be challenging the sensibilities of others by siting some of its passages.

Most Freemasons will be familiar with *Psalms 133*. Here, King David talks about how pleasant it is for Brethren to dwell together in unity and compares it to the precious ointment used to anoint Aaron, the first high priest of the Mosaic covenant. As beautiful as we find this bible verse, without some research, we may not understand the comparison. However, if you explore the Book of Exodus, you will discover a passage, where God is speaking to Moses on Mount Sinai. In Chapter 30, the recipe for the precious ointment is dictated to Moses, i.e.:

*Take also for yourself the finest of spices: of flowing **myrrh** five hundred shekels, and of fragrant **cinnamon** half as much, two hundred and fifty, and of fragrant **cane** two hundred and fifty, and of **cassia** five hundred, according to the shekel of the sanctuary, and of **olive oil** a hin. And you shall make of these a holy anointing oil, a perfume mixture, the work of a perfumer; it shall be a **holy anointing oil** . . . And you shall anoint Aaron and his sons, and consecrate them, that they may minister as priests to Me.*

The holy anointing oil; therefore is a complex mixture of myrrh, cinnamon, cane, and cassia suspended in olive oil. Each of these spices had its own distinct characteristic; some sweet, some sharp, some hot and some soothing. Once combined, the resulting anointing oil had its own unique characteristic that was above and beyond the characteristic of any one of its individual components.

The Psalm is telling us that as the spices are combined to form a truly divine product, so it is when Brethren dwell together in unity. The individual characteristics of each Brother, some sweet, some sharp, some hot and some soothing, combine to form a truly divine product. Therefore, the Lodge becomes stronger by the unique characteristics of each individual Brother.

These lessons taken from the ritual and the VSL provide rich and meaningful messages that can be shared in Lodge. These efforts provide not only education for the candidates and new Masons, but offer the Lodge opportunities to rethink their degrees in a new way.

Festive Boards

The Festive Board is an important adjunct to the Masonic meeting. It creates a convivial space for Brethren to conduct Masonic work outside of the formal constraints reserved for the Lodge room. Although, it should not be confused with a Table Lodge, which is essentially a Lodge Communication, it does have a structure and rules of etiquette.

Quite simply, it is a dinner that typically follows a regular communication of the Lodge but with a structure intended to make the most of this valuable time. Whereas, it may not be practical to hold a Festive Board following every communication, when properly planned and executed, it can be a frequent occurrence. The following is an outline of how some Lodges go about planning a Festive Board:

- Reserve one meeting a month for managing Lodge business and making Lodge plans. Typically, one meeting a month should cover most important Lodge business.
- Reserve the second communication for a short Lodge meeting followed by a Festive Board.
- The structure of the Festive Board may include the following components:
    - Place oblong tables in a horseshoe w/ WM and officers at the head table.
    - If possible, use tablecloths, silverware and China.
    - All Brethren should try to wear their finest attire.
    - If possible, arrange for table service or at least arrange family style food on the tables.
    - Start w/ a prayer then serve the food; all eat together.

- Give visitors and more venerable members the opportunity to speak by assigning them a topic, then ask them to give a toast relating to that topic. Example of toasts (change for every meeting):
    - To Brotherhood
    - To Wisdom
    - To Charity
    - To Harmony
    - To Strength

Just as an example, here is a toast to Brotherhood - *As a FC, we have taken an oath not to wrong, cheat, nor defraud a Brother, but rather to help, aid and assist him. It is surely a comfort to be among those who have taken such a vow. For this great gift that I have received through Freemasonry, I will always be grateful..... To Brotherhood Brethren. (Author unknown)*

- Some Lodges may already have a tradition of giving some well-established toasts dedicated to such notables as:
  - The Head of State
  - The Grand Master
  - The Deputy Grand Master
  - The District Deputy or Provincial Grand Master
  - Worshipful Master
  - All officers of the Lodge, Past and Present

- Finally, the last toast of the evening can be the *Tyler's Toast*, always a heartfelt conclusion of the evening.

Typically, a toast is a one-way communication of respect, esteem and goodwill, and is directed by those drinking the toast to the subject(s). The subject(s) of a toast will remain seated. There is another form of demonstrating esteem and mutual respect known as Wine Taking. This should always be under the control of the Master with an eye towards temperance. When the Master takes wine with the Brethren, *all* those in attendance will stand. The meaning behind the taking of wine is that each party stands and pledges fidelity to the other.

Whether it is Wine Taking or a formal toast, it is to be conducted in a formal and respectful manner. There is no joviality, but rather an opportunity to demonstrate respect for the subject of the toast in an atmosphere of fraternal esteem. (There is no "firing of cannons" as might be done in a Table Lodge setting.)

- Well in advance of the dinner, one Brother should be asked to prepare a topic for discussion and lead it off. During the course of the dinner, ask each of the Brethren to comment on the topic. The following are some thoughts that might inspire meaningful dialog among the Brethren:
  - A topic taken from *The 15 - Minute Philosopher*
  - Socratic Debate - a form of cooperative argumentative dialogue between individuals, based on asking and answering questions to stimulate critical thinking.
  - Black & White Chip – A Brother is forced to argue for or against an issue based on the color of chip he takes from a hat. (This tends to stimulate very interesting dialog.)
  - "Brother, share your talents with us" - Remember that anything we do in Masonry is really just a mechanism to get to know our Brothers better.

- Print a 5 x 7 card w/ an agenda to include topic(s) for discussion, toasts and songs with a copy set down at each place setting.

- Print out the lyrics for one or two masonic songs
  - "The Level and the Square" - Rob Morris
  - "Auld Lang Syne" is a typical closing song

- ➢ If someone plays an instrument or has a particular talent, have him give a short rendition during the dinner.

Finally, as mentioned in the Installation Ceremony, the gavel is the Master's emblem of Masonic authority and should therefore be with him throughout the dinner. The judicious use of the gavel will keep the dinner on track, making it an enlightening and enjoyable experience for all.

By the way, the Festive Board might be a good opportunity to invite members of the local community to take part in the joyful and enlightening aspects of our Craft. Remember, we want them to think of us as a resource and an indispensable part of the community. Furthermore, it is an excellent opportunity to get to know prospective members and involve your candidates. The evening of the Festive Board will afford the Brethren the opportunity to enjoy both the ritual of the regular communications as well as the social side of Freemasonry. Traditions and practices of individual Lodges vary and are one of the aspects that make Freemasonry so interesting. The format of the Festive Board will eventually evolve into an event that will reflect the culture and personality of the Lodge. You should allow it to morph and change until it becomes your own.

Additional Thoughts

Because there are so many variables in developing an enlightened Lodge the Brainstorming exercise followed by affinity analysis is most critical.

Getting Started in Your Lodge

Formal training as a Past Master begins as he progresses through the ranks as a Lodge officer. At each step, he will find himself getting closer to the East. Therefore, the Past Master's Framework identified above should be employed as soon as practical to give him the experience necessary to develop his Masonic career. In this way, when he becomes an IPM, he is likely to be well-versed in using the tools necessary for creating excellence in the Lodge.

For those, who have not yet been exposed to the Past Master's Framework, these skills can be learned in order to provide the confidence and encouragement required to invigorate and engage other Past Masters to participate. These skills will also enhance the involvement of other Brethren, as they learn tools and techniques that will not only benefit the Lodge but also improve their professional careers.

Start with Listening Skills and then gradually move on to other tools, one at a time, or as opportunities arise in the Lodge. As the Worshipful Master prepares his annual plan, he should include orientation and training in these skills.

Finally, just get started. As you continue to employ these tools to manage Lodge activities, you will develop a level of confidence that will allow you to manage more and more challenges. You will become known as someone who knows how to get things done.

TEMPLATES - SECTION V

The Past Master's Handbook Module Templates

Basic Facilitation Skills
(Module 1)

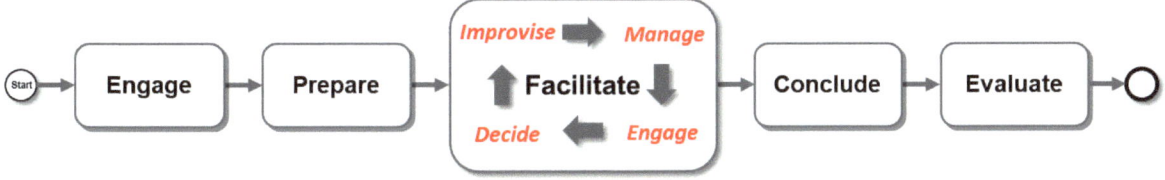

Lodge:	Date:
Purpose:	Participants:
Facilitator:	
Information	Analysis
Brainstorm Ideas: • • • • •	Themes/Categories: • • • •

Legend: Priority H (High), M (Medium), L (Low); QW (Quick Wins)

Statement of Work (SOW)

Prepared by:

Date:

Purpose:

Scope of Work:

Cost & Resources Needed:

Deliverables & Timeframe:

Agenda:

Authorization:

    Date:

    Worshipful Master_____

    IPM/PM_____

    Others_____

Running Order Agenda (ROA)
(Module 1)
Running Order Agenda

Lodge:	Date:
Purpose:	Participants:
Facilitator:	Other Support:

		Time
A	Opening and Background - Review Agenda & Logistics; Ground Rules; Introductions	
B	Agenda Item:	
	Break	
C	Agenda Item:	
D	After Action Review	
E	Next Steps	
	Wrap-up	

Participants' Agenda
(Module 1)

Lodge:	Date:
Purpose:	Participants: Facilitator:
Facilitator:	

A	Sponsor Kickoff	
B	Agenda Item(s)	
	Break	
C	Conduct an After-Action Review to Gather Feedback for Continuous Improvement.	
D	Next Steps	
E	Wrap-up	

Note: In the participants' agenda, identify only start time, break time(s), and end time. For each activity provide an estimated time. This way, participants don't notice the clock-time changes in the time flow, giving the facilitator flexibility to adjust as needed.

The Listening Ladder
(Module 1 a.)

Look	At the person speaking to you. Make eye contact to express that you are interested in what the other person has to say.
Ask	Questions. Ask follow-up open-ended questions to comprehend the meaning of what is being said by the speaker.
Don't	Interrupt or be interrupted. Ensure that the interruption is only for clarification of what has been said.
Don't	Change the subject. You will get an indication to change the topic when the speaker is finished with one thought. Look for cues to transition to another topic.
Empathize	With the speaker. Demonstrate this by a gesture such as "nodding your head" so that the speaker gets the message that you are interested in what is being said.
Respond	Verbally and nonverbally. Through body language such as nodding your head, eye/eyebrow movements, acknowledge that you are just as engaged in the conversation as the speaker is. You can do this without interrupting the speaker by saying, "…I see…" or "…I understand…"

With Active Listening	Speaker	Listener	Impression
Look			
Ask			
Don't			
Don't			
Empathize			
Respond			

Promotion Skills
(Module 1 b.)

Promoting the idea: _____(topic?)

1. Education

2. Collaboration & Consensus
.

3. Return-on-investment

4. Interpersonal skills

5. Persuasion skills

6. Organization

7. Social media

8. Keeping track

9. Meeting report

10. Communication

11. Timing

After Action Review
(Module 2)

Venue:	Date:
Topic & Scope:	Participants:
Facilitator:	Sponsor: Worshipful Master
I Liked	**I Wish**
Recommend Improvements:	

When finished, identify three to five top areas of improvement in the "I Wish" column with an Asterisk *. Assign someone to document the input collected.

Masonic Motivation
(Module 3)

Current Role/Assignment: _____

Quality	Current Role/Status	Score
Variety		
Adversity/Challenge		
Diversity		
Intensity/Depth		
Measure: Scale 1 to 10	Total	

Variety:

Adversity/Challenge:

Diversity:

Intensity/"Depth":

Transition to a desired role or responsibility:

Committee Charter

(Module 4 a.)

Name of Committee:	Type of Committee:	Date formed or authorized:

Purpose of Committee:

Authority:

Composition:

Meetings:

R - Responsible	
A - Accountable	
C - Consulted	
I - Informed	

Stakeholder	Message	Frequency	Mechanism	Who	When

Termination:

Lodge Performance Measures
(Module 5 a.)

Performance Measurement is the process of collecting, analyzing, understanding, and reporting information regarding the performance of a group or an organization, with the aim of ensuring sustainability and desired progress. In order to measure performance, one must first establish Key

Lodge Performance Measures:
Every Lodge can benefit by measuring the KPIs within the following areas:

Area	KPIs
(1) Membership	Active, dues paying, retention…
(2) Structure	Health of the line, succession planning, competency…
(3) Operations	Meetings, events, speakers, education, travel, charity, community events
(4) Finances	Income, expenses, assets, debt and physical structure
(5) Future Planning	Immediate and long term

For each of the agreed KPI's, an After-Action Review may be facilitated to determine what to measure.

KPI: _____

I Liked	I Wish

Priorities:

SWOT Analysis

(Module 5 b.)
SWOT (Strength, Weaknesses, Opportunities, and Threats)

Analysis is conducted for the current state of any organization or any part of an organization, including process, roles, products and services. A group brainstorming exercise is conducted with relevant stakeholders around the four quadrants as shown in the template **below**. The input is then identified into clusters of ideas (affinity analysis) to determine themes. The themes or items within the themes may be prioritized for action.

Note: **In some cases where an organizational entity may have many known problems, instead of SWOT Analysis, SPOT Analysis can be done the same way. SPOT: Strengths, Problems, Opportunities and Threats.**

STRENGHTS (Leverage)	**WEAKNESSES** (Convert into Strengths & Opportunities)
• •	• •
THREATS (Minimize & Convert into Opportunities)	**OPPORTUNITIES** (Leverage)
• •	• •

For Each Critical Item. Determine Implications:

ITEM
Implication / Consequences

Strengths	Weaknesses
ITEM **Implication** *Priority:*	**ITEM** **Implication** *Priority:*
Opportunities	**Threats**
ITEM **Implication** *Priority:*	**ITEM** **Implication** *Priority:*

SPOT Analysis

(Module 5 c.)

SPOT (Strength, Problems, Opportunities, and Threats)

SPOT Analysis may be facilitated just as shown in SWOT template. This template is an alternative approach for gathering brainstorming data. **(Note: SPOT Analysis may be conducted when the problems are serious and need attention relatively sooner).**

Greatest Strengths (Typically internal to the Area of Focus):

4. _____
5. _____
6. _____

Serious Problems (Typically internal to the Area of Focus):

4. _____
5. _____
6. _____

Greatest Opportunities (Typically external to the Area of Focus):

4. _____
5. _____
6. _____

Serious Threats (Typically external to the Area of Focus):

1. _____
2. _____
3. _____

Project Management
(Module 5d.)

Project Plan

---

1 – Project Name: 2 - Program Name:

3 - Description/Context:

---

4 - Scope/Deliverables:

5 – Organization/Communication Plan:

6 – Approach:

6 – Assumptions and Constraints:

6 – Financials:

7- Mile Stones:

#	Activity/Deliverable	When	Who	Status
1.				
2.				
3.				
4.				
5.				

8 – Close/Learnings:

Works Cited

After-Action Review, Continuous Improvement Made Easy, by Artie (Arjit) Mahal. Technics Publications. www.techicspub.com

Better Angels of our Nature, 2010, by Michael A. Halleran, University of Alabama Press

Bowling Alone, 2000, By Robert D. Putnam, Simon & Schuster Paperbacks

Encyclopedia of Freemasonry, 1884, by Albert G. Mackey, L.H. Everets & Co.

Facilitation and Training Toolkit, Engage and Energize Participants for Success in Meetings, Classes, and Workshops, 2014, by Artie (Arjit) Mahal, Technics Publications. www.techicspub.com

Illustrations of Masonry, 1829, by Willim Preston, Whittaker, Treacher, and CO.

King James Version of the Bible, 1611, Church of England

Masonic Manual & Code – 1947, The Grand Lodge F&AM of Georgia, The A.J. Showalter Co.

Monuments & Masons, On The Gateway To America, A Legacy of Freemasons, 2024, by Arjit S. Mahal.

Observing the Craft, 2010, by Andrew Hammer, Mindhive Books.

The 15 - Minute Philosopher, 2014, Arcturus Publishing.

The Freemason's Monitor, 1818, by Thomas Smith Webb, Cushing and Appleton.

The Constitutions of the Free-Masons, 1723, by James Anderson, *Printed by William Hunter, for John Senex at the Globe, and John Hook at the Flower-de-luce over-against St. Dunstan's Church, in Fleet-street.*

The Master's Book, 1974, by Carl H. Claudy, The Temple Publishers.

***The Old Past Master,* Hardcover,** 1924, Carl H. Claudy, The Masonic Service Association.

To Do Doing Done, 1997, by G. Lynne & Wycoff Joyce Snead, A Fireside Book by Simon & Schuster.

Notes

Notes

Notes

Notes

Notes

Notes

Notes

Notes

Authors

R.W. Robert W. Howard, Jr., PGH
Eclipse Lodge No. 67 (New Jersey, USA).

RW Brother Howard is a student of history, having previously served as Grand Historian. He is also a Past Master of New Jersey Lodge of Masonic Research and Education No. 1786. He has written a number of articles for the New Jersey Freemason, facilitated the Grand Lodge Mentoring program and has made numerous Masonic presentations to Lodges around the state. He holds an MBA in Marketing and has years of management experience with a number of sales and marketing organizations.

R.W. Arjit S. Mahal, PGC
LaFayette Lodge No. 27 (New Jersey, USA), Lodge Formanite No. 155 (India).

RW Brother Mahal served as a Grand Champlain in 2019. He is also a Past Regional Grand Steward in the Grand Lodge of India. He has been a Mason for the past 56 years and has served on various Grand Lodge Committees. Brother Mahal was appointed to various commissions by three governors of New Jersey: Thomas H. Kean, Jim Florio, and Christine Todd Whitman. He has many years of managerial experience with Mars, Incorporated, and was the founder of a private consulting firm. Brother Mahal has also authored several books.